THE GERMAN WOMAN

Servant or Companion

LENA WELLINGHUSEN

(First Edition 1922)

18th and 19th Thousand
1925
Ludendorff's Publishing House, Ltd., Munich
English Translation 2025 Invisible Empire Publishing
LLC Translation by Daniel Zakal

Trigger/Offensive Content Warning and General Disclaimer:

Dedicated to my children

CONTENTS

PREFACE

As the translator my goal has been to render the original German text into English with absolute fidelity, preserving its tone, structure, and intent without imposing modern distortions or reinterpretations. Every effort has been made to maintain the integrity of the author's voice, ensuring that what you read reflects their unfiltered ideas and expressions. This translation is not an adaptation but a bridge—one that allows the reader to engage directly with the text as it was written.

Understanding the Edda

Central to the author's arguments and worldview is the Edda, a foundational text of Norse mythology and Germanic heritage. For those unfamiliar, the Edda encompasses two primary works: the Poetic Edda, a collection of ancient Norse poems, and the Prose Edda, written by Snorri Sturluson. These works serve as a repository of the mythological and heroic traditions of pre-Christian Germanic culture. To the author, the Edda symbolizes an untainted connection to ancestral roots, embodying virtues like courage, self-reliance, and wisdom. It functions in this work as both a source of inspiration and a counterpoint to influences perceived as foreign or corrupting.

"Oriental" in Context

The term "Oriental," as used in this text, carries a specific and historically charged meaning. It does not refer strictly to a geographical region but rather to a set of ideas, values, and spiritual traditions the author views as alien to Germanic culture. This term primarily critiques the perceived imposition of Abrahamic religions—Judaism, Islam, and Christianity—on Germanic society. To the author, these "Oriental" influences represent a departure from what they argue is the natural harmony of Germanic blood, belief, and cultural identity.

The Historical Context and Translator's Approach

This book emerges from a period of intense political and ideological transformation in Germany. It reflects the author's alignment with völkisch (folk-centered) movements, which sought to revive what they regarded as the "noble" essence of Germanic culture. The arguments presented are unapologetically rooted in this worldview, often contrasting the author's idealized vision of

Germanic heritage with what they perceive as destructive external forces.

In translating this work, I have taken great care not to dilute or distort its content, even when the ideas expressed may challenge contemporary sensibilities. My role as a translator is not to judge or reinterpret the material but to ensure it is conveyed accurately and transparently. The author's tone, phrasing, and intent have been preserved to the greatest extent possible. Where necessary, annotations provide historical or cultural clarification, but these are strictly supplementary and do not alter the text.

CHAPTER

1

A MOTHERLESS PEOPLE

"Men make history!"

If this statement is only meant to refer to singular, outstanding personalities who powerfully influenced the course of world history and left their mark on centuries, then it is true. But in an expanded sense, it is equally valid. Indeed, for more than 1,500 years in our country—and in other nations for even longer—history has almost exclusively been shaped by men.

This fact bears significant responsibility for why history became so power-hungry, bloody, and cruel. It was inevitable that this would take its toll: the male-dominated leadership of a world designed for two genders worked against divine will. By depriving the people of the mother, the results—despite all the great gifts of men—could lead to nothing but decline in every area: politically, economically, culturally, and, above all, spiritually.

Just as a family cannot thrive without a mother or when her influence is undermined, neither can a nation. A nation, too, is a shared destiny, much like a family, and it requires both parents. Undoubtedly, a state predominantly or exclusively led by women would have likewise resulted in decline, albeit in a different way, than a state solely led by men. Man and woman are complementary entities. Their differences are ordained by God and nature. Where they work together, families and nations flourish; where only one parent has influence, they suffer and become orphaned.

We Germans are a people bereft of a mother. This is our deepest sorrow, from which all other misfortunes have followed.

But it was not always this way. A look into the past reveals a picture of our homeland as it once was—when the German woman could still be a mother to her people, when she stood as an equal beside the man, complementing his efforts to bring blessings to family and nation. How different things became when foreign ways, teachings, and ideas displaced or overshadowed the inherent value of Germanic womanhood. This shift caused the influence of women on public life to cease, confining it to the family and diminishing it even there due to her devaluation.

Over the centuries, our departed ancestors would tell us that the disenfranchisement of women and the exclusion of their influence on the people is the deepest cause of our decline.

Many Germans, raised with contempt for their ancestors, might respond: "The image of the past is obscure. The Germanic woman was prey, abducted and forced to work as a slave while the men amused themselves hunting or drinking mead." — Even though the prehistoric museums in major cities reveal that this is an outrageous lie, it continues to be systematically spread even today.

There is a very specific reason for this, one that becomes apparent to anyone who seeks the truth without prejudice. The purpose of this writing is to historically refute this lie and thereby serve the freedom and human dignity of German women and the restoration of the nation's health. May it help to return the mother to the German people.

CHAPTER

2

THE WOMAN IN
EARLY GERMANIC TIMES

As long as our people lived according to their natural, divinely ordained character, they were healthy. They were in harmony with the meaning of their existence. They thought, believed, and acted as their blood and inherent nature dictated. But over 2,000 years ago, when Roman ideas and customs penetrated the Germanic forests, things began to change.

A healthy people, rooted in nature, was poisoned by foreign influences. The poison acted slowly and insidiously. As long as the people retained their native faith, remained rooted in their past, and honored their ancestors, they were able to renew themselves through these traditions and largely preserve their natural way of life.

However, deep darkness descended upon the homeland about 1,000 years ago, when foreign influences also encroached upon their faith. When freedom of thought ceased, and the connection to the past was forcibly severed, the decline accelerated.

A fiery blaze in which the "pious" Louis burned all the poems and memories of our people's origins and past was likely our most fateful turning point. His father, Charles the Saxon-Slayer, the first pope-crowned "Roman Emperor of the German Nation," had carefully collected them. Once the knowledge of our own history was destroyed, falsehoods could complete their devilish work. Within just a few generations, German children could be deceived into believing that their ancestors were uncultured, half-naked savages and drunkards, and that the Germanic woman was merely the enslaved laborer of the man.

Yet there is a divine law that truth always triumphs, like the sun overcoming the darkest and longest night. And so, despite all destruction, slander, and the "pious" hatred, testimonies have survived that provide irrefutable evidence about the Germanic past.

One such piece of evidence is the burial site from 7,000 years ago. The native moorland and the coffin made from German oak have so faithfully preserved the dead of our people that their image comes alive before us once more today. It does not depict a barbaric people, but a people of high culture who, driven by a deep yearning for beauty, created noble art and dressed in harmony with their aesthetic sensibilities.

The burial also disproves another falsehood—the lie about the enslavement of the Germanic woman. It tells us that women, like men, were buried with weapons at their sides and alongside warriors. This is a clear sign that women, too, enjoyed personal freedom, dignity, and responsibility. They were not seen as mere maids and servants, but as equals, companions, and comrades-in-arms of men.

The grave speaks the truth. Prehistoric museums preserve it, and it is further confirmed by other evidence. German children should be familiar with this truth today. Another reliable source of such evidence is the Roman writer Tacitus. A single copy of his Germania was "accidentally" preserved by a monk in the oldest Benedictine monastery in northern Germany, the Corvey Abbey, saving it from destruction. Tacitus recounts the same truths as the grave. In his Germania, he writes:

"It is not the woman who brings a dowry to the man, but the man who brings one to the woman. These gifts are not frivolities, but livestock, a bridled horse, and a shield with frame and sword. The bride, in turn, presents the man with a piece of weaponry. Such gifts are considered the strongest bond, sacred customs of mysterious significance, and the protective deities of the marriage union. So that the wife does not think herself exempt from heroic spirit and the vicissitudes of war, the solemn beginning of her marriage reminds her that she comes to her husband as his companion in toil and danger, and that she is to share his fate and risks in war and peace as his free equal."

Tacitus, a Roman and an enemy of our people, surely did not intend to sing praises of us. His account is further corroborated by other records preserved in the sea-encircled Iceland. These are fragments of the Edda. The Edda speaks of as many goddesses (Asinnen) as gods (Asen). These luminous figures of Germanic antiquity, also called deities, were not worshipped as personal gods. They were poetic representations or embodiments of the racial characteristics of our people or the natural forces as they were understood at that time.

Tacitus writes: "It is not in the Germanic view of the divine to confine the heavenly beings within walls or to depict them with human features." This, too, refutes the Christian myth of our ancestors' supposed idolatrous worship. All the attributes of the Germanic woman were embodied in the goddesses (Asinnen), and they were regarded as equals to the gods (Asen).

The highest goddess, who united all the Germanic feminine qualities, was Freia, also known as Frigga or Frauja. From her, we derive the word "women" (Frauen). She is the loving, caring wife and mother who brings sunlight and warmth to the home, awakens joy, and gives life to laughing children. She is the tireless housekeeper who instills in the young an appreciation for the good, the true, and the beautiful, guiding them toward purity of morals and inspiring them with honor and heroism. She watches over loyalty and oaths, helps her people, and warns them of impending doom.

Beside her stand the goddesses of love, Minna and Loba, whose names survive today in "Minne" (love) and "Verlobung" (engagement).

Gaba, the goddess of the childless, shows women who must forgo the rich blessing of motherhood how they can find compensation for their hardship through generosity to the noble members of the community.

Heila, the healer, represents a role for which our ancestors believed women were particularly suited due to their nurturing and selfless motherly nature.

Lehna, the helper, provides advice and support to her people.

Our Ancestors 3,500 Years Ago
(Early Bronze Age)
Prehistoric Museum, Halle

"Verwahre", the goddess associated with justice, was appointed as a guardian in court proceedings to oppose one-sided and unjust judgments by men. This influence, too, was completely taken away from women.

Matz praises the moral prudence of the Germanic woman—her sense of moderation, which avoids everything offensive and excessive. Even in a 12th-century poem dedicated to her, **Maß** ("measure") is called the "model of all virtues." Many other examples could be cited.

Saga, the goddess of storytelling, is also a woman and symbolizes the art of narration, reflecting the Germanic woman's talent for epic storytelling. Like flowers that bloom and open their colorful petals under the sun, so did the luminous abilities of the Germanic woman flourish for her people as long as she was respected and held in equal esteem.

The heroic qualities of Germanic women are embodied by the **Valkyries**. They fight against enemies, free captives, protect heroes in battle, and escort them to Valhalla. They teach us that the Germanic woman must uphold heroism beyond death and carry it into future generations. The heroic fighting and dying of Germanic women were witnessed by the Romans during wars with northern peoples, and they reported on it with deep astonishment.

The *Edda* provides further evidence of the high regard for Germanic women, particularly in its creation myth. Unlike the Oriental myths, which depict women as being created inferior, the creation story of our blood presents women as equal to men, though fundamentally different in nature. According to the *Edda*, both men and women emerged from primitive stages of humanity, represented by trees—equal in value but of different kinds.

Man was created from the hard, unyielding wood of the ash tree, while the woman was formed from the soft, supple wood of the alder tree. Yet, our German children hear nothing of this marvelous Germanic metaphor of equality and distinctiveness between the sexes—a concept that portrays their divine differences as complementary, designed to balance and complete one another.

From this understanding, the Germanic people distributed the responsibilities of family and national preservation between men and women. The man, being harsher and more austere, with a strong will to power and a cooler, more calculating mind, was therefore best suited to shape life outwardly. The woman, being gentler and richer in emotion, deeper in her spiritual life, was thus best equipped to influence inwardly—on the soul of the child and the soul of the man.

This ability granted women the noble duty of awakening and strengthening the experience of the divine, thereby providing the people with moral stability through godly-directed striving. For our ancestors knew very well that moral purity is the backbone of a people. The *Edda* recounts that it is the Norns who sprinkle the World Ash Tree every morning with water from the Well of Becoming, which bubbles beneath its roots, so that it might grow and thrive. The World Ash Tree was a poetic representation of the Germanic religious worldview.

The Norns also spin the thread of eternity. The meaning of this myth is that the Germanic woman—rooted in the past of her people—understands the present and guides the path to a future that promises well-being for her people. She knew and proclaimed their history. Tacitus confirms what the *Edda* conveys, writing:

"The Germanic people attribute a sacred and elevated wisdom to women; thus, they follow their advice and seek their answers on matters of destiny. Under the reign of the deified Vespasian, we Romans still witnessed the prophetess Veleda, who was widely regarded as a divine being. Likewise, they had previously revered Albruna and others. Yet this was neither flattery nor deification."

The Germanic people understood very well that women, through their maternal instincts, perceive the dangers threatening their people more sharply than the more carefree, self-assured man. They knew that women, through their foresight, drew rich and extraordinary insights. Thus, they listened with gratitude and reverence to the advice of the mother.

For this reason, they also regarded women as better suited than men to serve as the spiritual awakener and proclaimer of the divine for their people. The strong will to power in men too easily led, in matters of religion, to arrogance and despotic priesthood. Yet the Germanic people's thirst for freedom neither tolerated nor endured priesthood. Their virtue had to be voluntary, independent of reward or punishment. Only then, in their view, was it of value.

"Good morals mean more to them than good laws do elsewhere," writes Tacitus.

Intelligent and curious, receptive to all that is beautiful and refined, the Germanic woman lived in a spiritual connection to God and nature, as reflected in the works of Dr. Mathilde Ludendorff. It is hardly possible for a people who granted their women such great dignity to simultaneously degrade them to the roles of servants, slaves, or beasts of burden. If such lies are still propagated today, despite better knowledge, the motives behind them are all too transparent.

This intrinsic Germanic reverence for women excluded both prostitution and polygamy. Contemporary accounts of Germanic peoples consistently confirm this. They praise the high morality of the Germanic tribes. Tacitus writes:

"Chastity is strictly observed in Germania, and in no respect do Germanic customs deserve greater praise," and: "The marriage bond among the Germans is strict; they are the only non-Romans who remain faithful to a single wife."

In sacred voluntariness, loyalty was given by both spouses. This required no vows, no kneeling before a priest, and no legal marriage contract. Loyalty does not tolerate coercion. When forced, it is worthless. Those who do not give loyalty freely will not keep it under compulsion either. And nothing is more unworthy of marriage partners than to monitor one another.

Our ancestors, of course, knew no double standard that permits men what it forbids women. Such a concept came to us with foreign influences. Polygamy reduces a woman from a partner in destiny to a mere plaything or slave. It is, like prostitution, a product of the desert cultures of the Orient, dishonoring both Germanic men and women alike. Many are trapped by it in lifelong, sorrowful mediocrity, harming the health of the nation. Dwelling in such lowlands renders them incapable of striving for spiritual and intellectual unity. Those who find comfort in the swamp are no longer drawn to the mountain air. In doing so, they rob themselves of life's holiest joy.

The moral self-control practiced by the Germanic peoples kept them healthy and strong. Tacitus reports:

"A young man comes late to experience love, preserving his unspent strength as a man. Similarly, the marriage of young women is not rushed. They live in the same way. Thus, young men and women come together only in the prime of their years, and the number of children testifies to the full vitality of the parents."

Julius Caesar, in his war accounts, also testifies to this, astonished and deeply impressed by Germanic purity of morals. He writes:

"The Germans regard it as disgraceful to approach the opposite sex before the age of twenty (the time of marriage). Yet they do not live apart. They bathe together in the rivers, dressed only in short furs."

The custom of late marriages persisted in our people for a long time. The poet of *Dietrichsflucht* (1260–1287) states that during the time of his hero Dietwart, neither man nor woman was allowed to marry before the age of thirty. Unfortunately, this is no longer the custom, and the world reveals the consequences. Similarly, Johannes Murner, 300 years later, laments this in his poem *Von Celichs Stadtsnuh und beschwerden* ("On Celich's Peace and Hardships"). The Christian era broke with this Germanic tradition.

The Nordic people mature later than Southerners and also remain young longer. Indeed, they retain the heart of a sun-loving child throughout their lives, provided vigilant, godly parents and educators preserve their natural essence.

The accounts of Tacitus and Caesar regarding the moral purity of the Germanic people are supported by other Roman writers. Procopius recounts that Totila had a Goth executed for behaving improperly toward a Neapolitan girl and gave the girl his wealth. Even the Roman bishop Salvianus of Massilia, writing in the fifth century, confirms the moral purity of the Germanic tribes, stating:

"Among the modest Germans, we (Roman Christians) are shameless. I would even go further: our lust offends the Germans. Among the Goths, there are no Gothic fornicators. Only the Romans, by general consensus, are allowed to be licentious among them. We (Roman Christians) cherish shamelessness, while the Germans curse it; we flee chastity, while they love it; fornication is considered a crime among them, excluding one from the community, while with us, it is regarded as a virtue."

And further:

"Where the Goths rule, only the Romans remain unchaste. Where the Vandals rule, even the Romans cease to be unchaste. Such is the strength of their zeal for moral purity and the strictness of their discipline—not only are they themselves chaste, but, to report something new, something incredible, something almost unheard of—they have even made the Romans chaste."

If the term *vandalism* is still used today to describe destructive fury, it is as deliberate a slander as the other lies about Nordic peoples. It originates from the same Jewish source of venom that spread atrocity propaganda about German soldiers during the last world war.

The further back we look in history, the higher the status of women—even in other cultures elevated by Nordic emigrants. For instance, Professor Delitzsch, in his second essay on *Bibel und Babel*, writes about the high regard for women in ancient Babylonian times, contrasting it with the biblical denigration of women.

The Roman writer Nicolaus of Damascus describes the Lycians:

"The Lycians honor women more than men, take their names from their mothers, and pass their inheritance to their daughters."

This is also confirmed by Herodotus in pre-Christian times. In his Roman History of Antiquity, Professor Mommsen writes:

"The woman stood as an equal beside the man—not, as in later Roman law, at the level of children."

This was during that pre-Christian era when, as Heinrich Heine triumphantly reveals in his *History of Religion*, "the Roman Hercules had not yet been consumed by the poison of the Orient."

In the Icelandic sagas, we see men and women living side by side in proud equality, as naturally derived from the Germanic principle of the equality of women. Free and self-assured, women played an active role in the home, the hall, and the feast hall. Both genders celebrated their shared festivals and sunlit days with unrestrained joy. They drank from the same horn and bathed together, as Caesar recounts.

Women presented their own cases in court, signed legal documents, managed their properties independently, attended the *Thing* (assembly), traded their goods at the shipyard, and undertook long journeys alone and unimpeded, even across the sea. They sailed armed with the Norsemen and participated in their seafaring ventures. Before us rises the image of a noble, bold race of women, characterized by supreme physical ability, agility, endurance, purity of soul and intention, foresight, generosity, honesty, sincerity, freedom, and naturalness, combined with feminine grace and beauty.

Procopius describes the tall, slender stature, fair skin, and blonde hair of Germanic women and notes that even the pampered Eastern Romans marveled at the beauty of Gothic and Vandal women. A defining feature of Nordic women was their long, blonde hair. Germanic women were proud of this adornment. Helge, the daughter of Throstin, was celebrated as the most beautiful girl in Iceland, thanks in large part to her golden hair, which shimmered like spun gold in the sunlight and enveloped her like a mantle.

It is rightly said that the love of Germanic people is experienced differently than that of other nations, as each people has its own inherent soul-life. Through achievement, the Nordic person sought to win the favor of their beloved. The Germanic woman loved in her man the friend, the confidant of her soul. Her love was not, like that of Southerners, a blazing emotion that quickly burned out, but a force rooted deeply in the heart. It often originated in the heart of the woman, and the man accepted it as a recognition of his nobility and deeds, reciprocating it with affection and loyalty.

The most beautiful songs of the *Edda*, the *Helgi Songs*, tell the story of Sigrun, the daughter of Hagen, and how she meets Helgi. From the first time she saw him, she loved him with all her soul. However, her father has promised her to another man. She pleads with Helgi:

"I am betrothed to the grim Hödbroddr, but you alone shall be my beloved. Yet I foresee the wrath of my family. In a few nights, Hödbroddr will take me home unless you save me and challenge him to a duel."

She spoke as her tormented heart dictated, and Helgi comforted her:

"Do not fear your father's wrath or the enmity of your kin; you shall live with me, for you are of noble birth."

Hödbroddr has gathered an uncountable number of ships and warriors, supported by Sigrun's father and brothers. They seek vengeance against Helgi, who has taken the bride. Helgi had abducted Sigrun to protect and stand by her. Helping defenseless women was a natural act of nobility for the Germanic man. Fearlessly, Helgi fights and defeats all his enemies; but Sigrun's father and brothers fall in the battle. Only one remains, Dag, who promises peace and whom Helgi spares—for Sigrun's sake.

Bride's joy and sorrow for the dead battle within Sigrun's soul. Helgi marries her, and she gives him sons, but Helgi does not grow old. Although the surviving Dag swore peace, the obligation of blood vengeance weighs more heavily on him. He kills Helgi in Odin's sacred grove and confesses his deed to Sigrun. He offers her a rich *wergild*—even half the kingdom—as restitution.

Sigrun rejects him with scorn. The brave Helgi is dead; what good are gold and possessions to her now? His grave mound covers him, but Sigrun finds no comfort, and Helgi no rest!

In the evening, Helgi comes riding and sends word for her to come to him. Sigrun descends into the grave mound, kisses her dead beloved, and laments:

"Your hands are icy cold, and you are soaked in red blood everywhere. How can I ever atone for this?"

Helgi answers:

"You alone are to blame. Each of your tears has fallen on my chest like blood, cold and heavy. But let no one sing me a dirge, even as they see my wounds, for the fair daughter of Hagen lies with me, the dead, in the grave."

At dawn, Helgi must leave and rides to Valhalla. Sigrun is left alone. Night after night, she waits in vain at the grave mound for her beloved. Soon, her heartache brings her death. Yet both live on in song, as long as German mothers sing and tell their children of Germanic heroes.

Love in the *Helgi Songs* is, of course, different from what is found in modern love stories. Among the Germanic people, it did not matter who confessed love first; women also enjoyed this freedom. The love of the Nordic man was neither a sentimental adoration nor a fleeting whim or a brief intoxication, as the Oriental loves. It grew slowly, was deep and quiet like the sea, pure and austere like the snow of the North. But when insulted or threatened, the restrained passion would break through all barriers—whether in men or women. This is what the Nordic sagas tell us.

Only a noble, honorable man could awaken admiration and love in a Germanic woman. If she respected him, she would follow him even without love, if her word or the interests of her family demanded it. However, if the man acted dishonorably, her love would freeze, and she would leave him.

Geirmund abandoned Thurid and their one-year-old daughter without providing her with money to care for the child. Thurid had a ship prepared, sailed after him, and, under the cover of night, moored near his anchored ship. To prevent Geirmund from pursuing her, she ordered his ship to be sabotaged. While everyone was asleep, she placed their child on his bed, took his sword, and left him. Geirmund woke and called out to her, begging her to return his sword, promising her plenty of money in exchange. But Thurid replied:

"You shall never get it back, for you have behaved dishonorably toward me in many ways, and so it must end between us!"

Later, Thurid married Gudmund. Of her, it was said: *"She was a good woman, of noble spirit and exceptional character."*

In the Icelandic sagas, there are instances where a man forgets himself so far as to strike his wife. She avenges the blow or files for divorce, and she is granted justice; for the healthy Germanic sense of justice forbade men from abusing their physical superiority in such a way. Such brutality was abhorrent. The heroic Germanic man fought only against opponents of equal physical strength. To attack the weak or defenseless was considered cowardly and despicable.

It was a beautiful and wise Germanic custom not to give daughters a dowry. This ensured that they were desired not for their wealth but for their personality.

Germanic marriage was not a purchase agreement, and the bride was not a commodity to be traded, though it is still often misrepresented as such today. Instead, the dowry was brought by the man as a wedding gift to his bride, and it remained her property until her death. Only later, during the Christian era, did the concept of trousseaus emerge.

To protect women, they were assigned a *Muntwalt* ("guardian"). The word *Munt* means protection, not guardian in the sense of someone having authority over them, as it is often incorrectly interpreted. Before marriage, the father held this role; if he died, it passed to the brother; in marriage, it became the husband's responsibility.

In exchange for his guardianship (*Muntrecht*), the husband had a partial claim to his wife's inheritance. However, this right was revoked if he treated his wife dishonorably. For this right of guardianship, the husband paid a sum of money, which was not a purchase price for the bride but rather compensation for being entrusted with managing her inheritance. The Christian myth of marriage as a form of purchase is refuted by the legal historian Richard Schröder, who writes:

"The prevailing rule is that no woman could be married against her will."

Similarly, the prehistorian Professor Necke states:

"The girls were in solidarity with their family, acting only rarely outside of its agreement, but they were not subservient to their male relatives."

Legal history mentions Raubehe (marriage by abduction) as the oldest form of Germanic marriage. Tacitus, the earliest authority, does not mention it, but it undoubtedly occurred. If the "voice of the blood" spoke, as in the case of Hermann and Thusnelda, and the bride consented, such an abduction cannot be considered a crime. Among the Frisians, the abducted woman was placed between her parents and the abductor. If she turned to him willingly, all was forgiven. However, if she was taken against her will, such an act was punished as one of the most heinous crimes.

According to Icelandic law, not only the abductor but also any accomplice faced severe penalties and the vengeance of the family. The farther north one went, the purer the customs, as racial purity was preserved longer in these regions. Iceland, due to its isolation, retained Germanic traditions the longest. By the age of 20, Icelandic women had full control over their property, and even after marriage, this remained unchanged.

The Norwegian Forstathing law states:

"Both men and women retain control over their property as long as they have the strength to sit in the high seat of the house."

In property transactions conducted by women, their signatures appeared first on the documents under Alemannic, Salic, and Lombardic law.

The equal status of Germanic women is also evident in the Wehrgeld (compensation payment) for a killed woman, which was equal to that for a man. Some tribes even valued offenses against women more highly than those against men, demanding higher compensation—twice as much among the Bavarians and Alemanni, and three times as much in some cases.

Germanic nobility and virtue required helping and protecting women. It was only during the Christian era—under the influence of the Church—that the value of a woman was reduced to as little as one-third that of a man.

Because the role of the Germanic woman extended beyond the home, she was also prepared for her great responsibilities toward family and people. She participated in the high culture of her time. She recounted the heroic deeds of her people and inspired others with them. She learned and taught the singing of serious and joyful songs. She carved and interpreted runes, inscribing them on wood (*Buchs*, meaning "letters"), stone, and metal. She expressed her sense of beauty through crafting and weaving elegant garments. She adorned the home and hall, skillfully and artistically organizing festivals with games, songs, and dances.

She was prepared for her sacred role as a mother, being made aware, like young men, of the great responsibility to give her people healthy children and to maintain her body and soul pure and strong for this purpose. She safeguarded the morals and purity of her people, offered advice, and provided care. She healed the sick and wounded.

The *Glum Saga (Thule XI)* recounts:

"Hallorda brought women to the battlefield in Glum's fight against Thorarin, saying, 'We will bind the wounds of the men who still live, no matter which side they are from.' But when she arrived, Thorarin was struck down by Mar; his shoulder was torn away, exposing his lungs. Yet Hallorda bound his wounds and stayed with him until the battle ended."

Women also learned the use of weapons, as they needed self-defense even more than men. The mother handed the sword to her son, but hanging in her own home were a dagger and shield, symbols of her readiness to defend herself.

Thus, she was the strong companion of the man in life and destiny, sharing joy and danger with him both at home and in battle. Highest duties and highest rights were shared equally, forming a life-affirming partnership of active joy.

Even in the early centuries of the Roman-Christian era, men and women lived together in this way, as accounts from Tacitus, Caesar, Procopius, Plutarch, and Salvianus reveal. This shared leadership of men and women fostered a prosperous and happy people, as described by the historian Paulus Diaconus when speaking of the Germanic Lombards:

"And indeed, it was marvelous in the realm of the Lombards: No violence was committed, no secret conspiracies were formed. No one was unjustly forced into servitude, no one plundered. Theft and robbery did not occur. Everyone could live as they pleased, without fear or worry."

In their connection to God, the Germanic nature peoples—*"equal only to themselves"*—respected their moral laws in sacred voluntariness, without commandments. They lived the morality that arises from a German understanding of God. They sought perfection through their own strength—not through redemption—as the noble nature of the Germanic soul demands.

The Germanic people did not shy away from life-threatening tasks out of fear of suffering or desire for happiness, willing to "prevent worse" when fate presented them with difficult decisions, no matter how painful the path ahead might be. This is what German heroic sagas tell us, drawn from the lived experiences of their men and women.

Since this writing is devoted to the revival of the proud, noble Germanic woman, let us especially highlight the women.

Brunhild! Only the bravest, most fearless hero, Siegfried, could claim Brunhild. Reluctantly, she followed the Burgundian king, still respecting his courage as a man. But when she discovered that he had won her through deceit and betrayal, the bond was broken. Neither power, splendor, nor the crown of the Burgundian queen could compel Brunhild to endure a life without dignity. She avenged the humiliation she suffered and atoned for her revenge with voluntary death.

Riding Siegfried's horse, Grane, she leaped into the sea of flames that consumed him. Deliberately and with purpose, she prepared this end. *Better to die than live in disgrace!* Such is Brunhild's belief.

Krimhild! She held the dead Siegfried in her lap, the dearest thing the earth had ever borne for her. The *Edda* recounts of her:

"Yet Krimhild did not weep. So great was her pain, yet Krimhild could not and would not cry."

Only when Siegfried's wounds were uncovered did her tears break forth like a torrent.

Gudrun! Abducted by the son of a foreign king, she is promised splendor, power, and wealth if she accepts his proposal. Yet Gudrun prefers to endure years of humiliation and perform the hardest labor, never forsaking her loyalty. For thirteen years, Gudrun waits for her betrothed to bring her back to her homeland. With the same loyalty, her beloved spends those years devoted entirely to her liberation.

The enemy, the Norman duke, is likewise marked by greatness, purity, and nobility of spirit. He loves Gudrun but does not force himself upon her, granting only what she offers freely, even though she is in his power. Such an atrocity was inconceivable in Germanic thought.

The *Gudrunlied* is a sublime depiction of unshakable Nordic loyalty and a symbolic tale of the German woman's destiny. Like Gudrun, the German woman was also degraded to the status of a maid and servant by foreign influences and powers, and she now waits for the German man to bring her home again—to her once exalted position within family and people, to the honor and freedom of the Germanic woman!

Thusnelda in the "Triumphal Procession" of Germanicus
C. von Piloty

Eigne! Wälsung's sunny daughter, bound in a tormenting marriage to the dark, hate-filled, envious King Siggeir, whom she followed for her father's sake. He treacherously and vilely destroys her entire clan. Only one brother escapes into the forest. The heavy duty of family vengeance falls upon Eigne, a responsibility that our ancestors carried out with such harrowing resolve, subordinating all their desires for happiness to this task.

Eigne raises two sons by Siggeir. Though they resemble her outwardly, they inherit the dark, envious nature of their father. Her deepest sorrow is realizing the curse of mixing bloodlines in her own offspring. She knows these sons will never fulfill the vengeance. Thus, she sends them to their certain deaths and secretly gives herself to her brother to bear a true Wälsung—a child who will become her avenger and liberator.

After achieving family vengeance, freedom and happiness beckon Eigne. But guilt weighs heavily upon her. She cannot forget her betrayal of her husband, and this breach of loyalty demands atonement. It compels her to part from all the earthly joys still left to her, including the happiness reaching out to embrace her. She returns to the burning house and voluntarily meets her death in the flames. In death, Eigne attains perfection through self-redemption. Yet she failed to realize that even loyalty can become immoral.

Loyalty is a defining characteristic of the Germanic people, but it often became their undoing, as well as that of their nation, because it was held blindly. A word once given was seen as binding, even when it became clear that it was tethered to someone unworthy, strengthening forces opposed to the divine.

Our enemies have often exploited "German loyalty" to their advantage, binding German people with oaths that were deemed unbreakable by their sense of loyalty, leading to the spiritual destruction of individuals and the downfall of the nation. Loyalty is only moral when it serves what is noble and divine.

It is not only the heroes of myth who lived such grandeur and nobility. This greatness repeatedly shines throughout German history. Let us consider Hermann, to whom we owe so much. Without Hermann, there would long be no Germany. Rome knows this too—it has never forgotten the Teutoburg Forest. At the lavish Roman court, wealth and luxury were assured for Hermann if he betrayed his homeland. But he remained loyal, becoming its savior and avenger.

The same greatness lived in Thusnelda. Despite the hatred of her entire clan, she became Hermann's wife. Shared thoughts and feelings for their homeland, threatened by Rome, united their souls. She rose above her father, Segestes, who envied Hermann's ducal mantle, became a Roman ally, and handed his own daughter over to the enemy.

This is the deep tragedy in the life of our people since Roman influence penetrated the Germanic forests: alongside every Hermann, there has always been a Segestes, a traitor to his friend and homeland.

Rome hoped to break Hermann by enslaving his wife, but for Hermann, the fate of his homeland was greater than his own deepest suffering. He continued to fight, so that Rome forever abandoned its plans to return with the sword.

The Pinakothek in Munich preserves a painting that, in its solitude and grandeur, speaks to Thusnelda's harrowing fate and deeply moves the German soul. There is much the German people could learn from it. Even Caesar himself wanted to witness the triumph over the captured Germanic woman. Yet his jubilation was silenced, and his gaze fell before the pride, regal dignity, and defiant disdain of this one German woman in chains—who carried her cruel fate with such mastery and majesty.

"Her pain was silent; she shed no tears nor offered pleas," writes Tacitus. Unfortunately, Tacitus's *Annals* "coincidentally" omit the sections that would provide insight into Thusnelda's later fate. We can only assume what the German poet Friedrich Halm movingly recounts in his tragedy *The Gladiator of Ravenna*. Unfortunately, it never found its way to German stages. Germans, after all, are quick to ridicule their own. It is true that such greatness and majesty scarcely suit the theater of today.

Friedrich Halm tells us: Thusnelda's young son is taken from her by the Romans and raised as a gladiator, a fighter. She does not see him again until he is a young man. How she had yearned for that day all those years! How deeply it pains her to realize that her son has become a stranger to her. He knows nothing of homeland or fatherland, and he scarcely understands his mother's language. How could he, having rarely heard its sound over the years? Only one thing remains German within him: his courage in battle.

But it is not to free his mother or avenge his homeland that he wishes to fight. No, he seeks to distinguish himself as a Roman gladiator before Caesar. The mother tries in vain to persuade him to escape with her. She knows his fate. So, she kills her sleeping son and then herself. Her German pride saved him from falling before Caesar's eyes, as the sadistic Roman hatred had planned. Rome's emperor triumphed over corpses.

When Roman gladiators entered the arena, they knew few, if any, would leave alive. They saluted Caesar with their right hands and the cry: *"Ave Caesar, morituri te salutant"* (*Hail, Caesar, those who are about to die salute you*).

And when the Nordic crusaders marched into the Asian desert to liberate the grave of a Jew, they also knew that only a few would ever see their homeland again. They saluted the Roman bishops with the same gladiatorial cry.

Why are German children told so little—or nothing at all—about the greatness of their ancestors? Wouldn't the eyes of young German girls shine brightly if they were told of this noble German woman? Wouldn't her example fill them with strength and a will to triumph, enabling them to master any fate in life and grow into the dignity of Germanic womanhood? Or should the example of Sarah and Rebekah accomplish this better?

And what about the German boys, who hear of Hermann fleeing the opulent Roman court to save his homeland, uniting the Germanic tribes and making them victorious and invincible? Wouldn't this ignite courage and deep devotion to their people and homeland, making them more heroic than the example of biblical Jews? Those stories may hold value for Jewish children, but what relevance do they have for our German youth?

A group of boys who deeply understood the profound destiny of Hermann would never stoop to such ancestral mockery as German students do when they sing:

"And his wife Thusnelda drank like a house servant,"

to justify their excessive drinking.

Is this how the greatest and purest German woman is portrayed to the male youth?

Give our German children their history as a sacred book—not in dry dates or the lifeless memorization of battles and imperial lineages, nor in blind ancestral glorification. Instead, it should highlight the noble virtues and fatal flaws of the German racial heritage, inspiring admiration for greatness and nobility, while teaching serious lessons for the future through the recognition of past mistakes.

"Better to die than be a slave"—so thought the Germanic woman. Roman writers confirm this. Plutarch writes about the Roman battles with the Cimbri and Teutons:

"In the wagon fort, the women fought for a long time, their golden hair streaming in the wind, battling the Romans and even their own retreating men. When they saw everything was lost, they killed their children and then themselves. None surrendered to captivity."

Indeed, a people with such women was invincible. Rome knew this, as did the Jew, who, even at that time, was, as the historian Mommsen describes, *"the ferment of national decomposition."* In simpler terms, the seed of decay, which had already begun to corrode and degenerate the Latin peoples. The Judaized Rome clearly saw that these heroic peoples of the North could not be defeated by the sword, nor could they be bought with money. Therefore, other methods and means had to be devised to bring them down—spiritual weapons!

And Rome devised them, for it understood:

> "Watchful are the fair-haired hounds
>
> and they scorn money and riches.
>
> Do not attempt with such means
>
> to subdue the need-poor North.
>
> If you want to enslave their bodies,
>
> you must first murder their souls."

CHAPTER

3

THE GERMAN WOMAN UNDER SYNAGOGUE LAW

Thus, instead of the sword, Rome brought the cross into the Germanic forests to impose upon the German people the same fate that had already destroyed it. The Jewish poet Heine understood the causes of the decline of the once-heroic Roman people. He wrote:

"Indeed, Rome, the Hercules among nations, was so effectively consumed by Jewish poison that helmet and armor fell from its withering limbs, and its battle cries turned into the whining of praying priests."

Mussolini recognized this as well when—before the war, still a follower of Nietzsche—he confronted Vandervelde in Geneva, who spoke of the socialist ideas of the Redeemer and the sacred Communism. Mussolini correctly responded:

"Jesus and his disciples are guilty, for they undermined the structure of the mighty Roman Empire. They destroyed the strength and courage that made Rome great and the Romans immortal. Instead of strength, courage, and masculinity, they elevated humility, poverty, and peace to the throne of the Caesars. The morality of slaves! And the once-mighty Rome was poisoned by these servile teachings and no longer able to resist the flood of barbarians breaking in from the North. This is what I accuse Christ of."

In 1929, Mussolini publicly declared:

"If Rome had not adopted Christianity, Christianity would have remained an Oriental sect."

The church historian Dr. Wolf wrote in the same vein:

"Moses' chair came to Rome as Peter's chair."

Decaying Rome, corrupted by the blood and spirit of the Orient, trembled before the blond giants who, driven by their yearning for the sun, repeatedly stormed over the Alps. Rome saw no other way to fend them off than to carry north the very teachings that had so effectively destroyed the strength and heroism of the Romans.

It is hardly a coincidence that during the time when the entire Germanic North rose in all its tribes against Rome and achieved great victories, a council of priests was convened in Nicaea (325 AD) to determine which of the eighty gospels, all written by Jews, were to be considered *"divine revelation."* Four were selected and combined with the Jewish family history of the Old Testament into a single, inseparable book. With this, Judah had found the weapon that would make it the ruler of the world, as Moses had promised. With this weapon, it also conquered the Germanic forests.

Shrouded in the cloak of night, priests came to our sunlit homeland, bringing their crucified god. They sang, as if with heavenly harps, of *"peace on earth and goodwill toward men,"* and they whispered like dove voices: *"Blessed are the merciful, blessed are the peacemakers, blessed are the meek."*

Such songs ingratiated themselves with the loving, peace-filled German soul. Naive, unsuspecting, and trusting, it listened to them. Yet many rejected the foreign teachings. To them, it seemed too meek, too submissive, and even destructive to the people to *"love your enemy,"* to *"bless those who curse you,"* and, when struck, to *"turn the other cheek."* They rejected the new faith, which sought to redeem them from their tribe and people, and instead held fast to their own ways of thinking, which gave them courage, strength, and pride in their connection to God.

They did not think it possible that anyone could take away their freedom of spirit, which they so freely granted to others. They were soon to learn that Christian mercy and neighborly love did not apply to them. Instead, they were met with songs full of hate and enmity, which even divided families, setting sister against brother, children against parents:

"He who does not hate his father and mother cannot be my disciple."

For all the strong, upright, and loyal in the land, cruel commands were issued:

"But those enemies of mine who did not want me to reign over them—bring them here and kill them in my presence."

These commands gave degenerate Germans a clear conscience to rage against their own blood and their own people. Furthermore:

"I have not come to bring peace, but the sword."

"I have come to cast fire upon the earth, and how I wish it were already kindled."

And indeed, the flames burned again and again, even into the most recent times.

Jesuit General Francesco Borgia declared at the end of the 16th century about his order:

"We have crept in like lambs, we will rule like wolves, we will be driven out like dogs, and we will renew ourselves like eagles."

Once again, a god-inspired Germanic seeress warned her people not to abandon their ancestral faith. Thiota, from Alemannia, cautioned:

"Do not let the foreign god enter; he signifies the end of the world."

The people listened to her, for at that time, the Jewish Paul's decree—"*I do not permit a woman to teach*"—had not yet been enforced. Roman priestly hatred silenced Thiota. The bishops in Mainz sentenced her to the most dishonorable death a woman could endure. She was stripped naked and whipped to death.

The history of the "religion of love" is written in blood. We think of the Alemanni, murdered by the thousands in Cannstatt; of the 33-year resistance of the Saxons, who repeatedly rallied around their Duke Widukind because they refused to abandon their Germanic faith; of the brave Frisian farmers against whom all the lowly rabble was summoned for a crusade; of the thousands of German heroes lured to the deserts of the Orient for the sake of foreign ideas, where they perished or fell; of the children's crusades, whose victims were sold into slavery in Africa; of the millions of German kin annihilated in the 30-year struggle over faith; of the countless people who were burned alive or perished in dungeons for their free thinking.

We remember them and will not forget them!

Count Hoensbroech wrote:

"The path of the papacy is a path of horror and terror. On either side, it is lined with thousands of stakes and thousands of blood-soaked scaffolds."

The Germanic peoples had no priesthood that proclaimed doctrine as unshakable truth and was paid to do so. Nor did they worship a personal god. They lived in divine connection with a god-filled universe. Women were the ones who guarded the experience of the divine among the people. This, of course, could not be tolerated by priests, who came as representatives of Jehovah—that Jehovah who preached neighborly love yet tolerated no other beside himself. Women rendered priests unnecessary. They also safeguarded the moral integrity and purity of the people. A morally pure people, however, has no need for redemption.

Thus, the position of women in family and society had to be disrupted, as it did not align with the new doctrine. The new teachings spoke of women in ways entirely different from the Germanic worldview.

The desert is hostile to life; it brings forth no life and hates life. A doctrine born of the desert must, therefore, also hate women as the bearers of nascent life. This is consistent with its origins.

The fertile, life-filled, child-loving Germanic land, however, viewed celibacy as unnatural. In the Jewish creation story, the woman is not equal to the man, as in the myth of our people—no, the woman is inferior.

German children are not taught the creation myth of their own bloodline. Nor are they told about the scientific understanding of the development of all living beings, from single cells to humans. Where this is occasionally taught, there is complete silence about the divine meaning that Dr. Mathilde Ludendorff, the philosopher of the soul, conveyed in her works on the soul. She spoke of the ascent from unconscious primordial cells, through plants and animals, to the god-conscious human being.

Instead, German children are still taught today that the world was created by the almighty "Let there be" of an extra-worldly, personal god, in the pace of a six-day sprint, where trees and grass grew even before a sun was hung in the sky.

Well, the Jewish storytellers were apparently poor farmers even back then.

The first human was formed from clay, but there wasn't enough clay left to create a companion for Adam. However, he wasn't meant to be alone. So Jehovah took a rib from Adam—after presumably putting him to sleep—and transformed and extended it into something else. From this rib came a beautiful Eve, over whom Adam was so delighted that he, at least in this regard, forgot the painful procedure and was very happy with the transformed rib in paradise.

But the joy was not to last long. Nietzsche writes:

"Jehovah grew tired of always being God, so he lay down as a serpent under a tree and seduced Eve."

The serpent showed Eve a beautiful apple and told her it would make her wise. Wisdom, thought Eve, is a good thing, and so is an apple. So she ate the apple. In her generosity—characteristic of women or at least as it should be—she gave some to Adam as well. Adam, lacking willpower, did not refuse the apple but ate it happily. After all, he didn't want to remain foolish, even if eternal bliss was promised to him in exchange.

And so the terrible calamity occurred, under which we all still suffer to this day. Eating the apple in paradise became the turning point of humanity's fate! This is original sin, which weighs like a curse on humanity to this day because sin had thus entered the world. And Eve alone is to blame for it, even though Adam ate as well.

Adam even shifted the blame onto Eve himself:

"The woman whom you gave to be with me gave me fruit from the tree, and I ate."

This, of course, is something Siegfried would never have done!

Thus, Eve had to be punished for bringing sin into the world. And how was she punished? Her most sacred, natural role—her role as a mother—was defiled as a punishment:

"With pain, you shall bring forth children."

As if all creation is not accompanied by pain! As if the entire universe was not born in the most terrible convulsions! Are not all works of genius born from the deepest turmoil of the soul? How could it be otherwise with nature's highest masterpiece—a child?

To interpret it this way, one must possess the swampy imagination of the Orient, which also concludes that childbirth is something impure, requiring the mother to first cleanse herself. Furthermore, Moses declares that giving birth to a girl renders the mother impure for 30 days longer than giving birth to a boy. Only after she has offered a sacrifice to the priest can she be considered a full human being again.

"The Church is a cash register," writes Victor Hugo.

The sinful woman can only bring forth sin, they argue. Thus, every human is sinful because they are born of a woman. Since women are considered inferior and sinful, they must be subjugated by men. As it says in the Old Testament:

"Your desire shall be for your husband, and he shall rule over you."

And in the New Testament:

"Wives, submit yourselves to your husbands, as to the Lord. For the husband is the head of the wife."

The Jew Peter adds:

"Wives, submit yourselves to your husbands in the Lord, as is fitting."

"Let the woman be subject to the man who has authority over her."

And again:

"In the same way, wives should submit to their husbands."

Every German woman kneeling before the priest on her wedding day must hear these words from him. If she bore them patiently, it was because her soul, when faced with the beloved man, becomes childishly soft and pliant, willingly submitting to his wishes and yielding to his leadership.

On the other hand, the German man rarely exercised the rights granted to him over his wife, for the heroic German does not subjugate women. Only those who are themselves slaves—who bow before church officials, superiors, or secret lodge leaders, and have thus lost their own human pride—seek to oppress women and cannot tolerate pride in others.

To further prevent a spiritual bond between man and woman, enmity must be sown between them. Divide and rule!

"Because you listened to the voice of your wife, cursed is the ground because of you."

Where man is the friend of woman, the priest as a "soul shepherd" becomes unnecessary. The woman reveals her soul to her beloved man, not to the foreign, celibate priest. But the priest must always be present, for he determines the number of children and much else. Therefore, discord must be sown, and men must be taught to despise and subjugate women. Only then can they be lured into secret societies, only then can they be corrupted.

So, the woman is considered inferior, burdened with original sin, and impure. So impure that even in the Middle Ages, she was only allowed to touch the host while wearing gloves. So impure that the priest was not supposed to touch her:

"Concerning the matters you wrote to me about, I reply: It is good for a man not to touch a woman."

What Paul continues to say about marriage is so vile that it cannot be repeated here. The German woman should read it for herself and then ask whether, for the sake of cleanliness and her dignity, she should continue living under synagogue law or instead make use of the right to leave the church, granted to Germans by Bismarck in 1873 for their liberation.

Because women are viewed as so sinful, impure, and inferior in Christian doctrine, priests at the Council of Nicaea debated for weeks whether women even had souls. By a narrow margin of just one vote, it was decided that women did indeed have souls—otherwise, they would have been classified alongside animals, to whom the Jew denies a soul. Even as late as the 18th century, councils were still debating whether women were fully human. To proclaim the word of God, they first had to don women's clothing themselves to achieve holiness.

One such enlightened man argued that a female fetus receives its soul 40 days later than a male fetus. Another claimed that no angel has ever appeared as a woman and therefore only men can be angels. Peter did not allow impure women into heaven, and thus women must first become men at the resurrection. For those women who value the promise of resurrection, this is at least a comforting prospect—that they may transform into a state of glory.

Because women are considered so inferior and impure, priests must remain celibate. The unnatural nature of this command led to terrible degenerations among the once morally pure German people, with effects that remain unpunished to this day. Indeed, this is the most effective weapon for destroying nations. Immoral individuals and peoples lack defenses. They can be dominated and even used for the most terrible crimes.

Girls, too, are advised to remain celibate, albeit for different reasons. Only as brides of Christ can they be redeemed from their original sin. Tragically, it was often the earnest, God-seeking individuals who were lost to the nation in this way. Should nature triumph and a child be born, the young life was often destroyed, as evidenced by the countless skeletons of infants found in convents.

If everyone were to follow the discipline of desert asceticism, there would soon be no people left to rule. But servants are needed. Therefore, a woman's value must be measured solely by her ability to bear children:

"She shall be saved through childbearing."

Even though she is otherwise considered the bearer of all vices in the world, she is indispensable for procreation—otherwise, there would soon be no men either. Thus, the greater the number of children, the more "worthy" the woman.

This logic ignores the fact that women who cannot have children can also make valuable contributions to their people. Furthermore, such an assessment leads to the exploitation of women's health and physical strength. At the same time, it ensures that women can no longer fulfill their sacred duty of spiritual care for their family and community. A woman so overburdened, particularly in today's economically strained times, has no strength left to provide moments of celebration for her family.

She has likely not yet realized that *"the heavenly Father feeds them all."* She knows that even the lilies of the field only grow if they are rooted in fertile soil.

Many believe that the Church's terrible contempt for women is counterbalanced by the veneration of Mary. They fail to see that Marian veneration actually represents the opposite of honoring motherhood. Only the woman who is said to have conceived unnaturally is revered; only she alone is considered pure. Women likely do not realize what an insult this is to every woman and mother. This veneration aligns with the Jewish notion of the impurity of the senses, of creation, and of childbirth. It contradicts Germanic sensibilities. According to the Edda myths of our ancestors, everything drawn from the wellspring of creation was of divine purity.

Two white swans, they said, silently traced their eternal circles upon the waters of the Ard-well. Through Jewish soul-poisoning, this holy spring has been turned into a frog swamp, and the swans into the stork that fetches children from the mire. Since then, German parents have been ashamed to give their children true answers to serious and sacred questions. Curious children then seek these answers elsewhere, often from inappropriate sources, and are corrupted by them. The mother is best equipped to answer her child's questions—appropriately for its age—better than the dishonorable priest who views sacred creation as impure.

Furthermore, early Christianity did not recognize Marian veneration. The Bible itself makes no mention of it. On the contrary, Jesus says to his mother:

"Woman, what have I to do with you?"

This hardly sounds like honoring one's mother.

Biblical contempt for women has deprived our people of the mother. We know how sorrowful a motherless family is and that it cannot thrive. A motherless people is equally sorrowful. Fortunately, respect for mothers is ingrained in the blood of Germans, so much so that it continues to live on in the majority today. For this, Germans did not require a commandment promising rewards, as was the case with the Jews.

The Germanic reverence for *Frauja* found poetic expression. When the Germans refused to relinquish their *Frauja* reverence, along with their festivals like Christmas, Ostara, and High May Day, these were altered and Orientalized, just as their sacred celebrations were.

According to the myths of our ancestors, *Frauja* stood in the crescent moon, holding her little daughter in her arms—a child named Kleinod after her father, Od. Because she was so beautiful, anything charming or precious has since been called Kleinod in her honor. *Frauja* was transformed into the Jewish Mary, and Kleinod into the Jewish Jesus.

If today Nordic faith communities attempt to reverse this process by transforming Mary back into *Frauja* to rekindle bonds among awakening Germans, such efforts will be as ineffective as attempts to portray Jesus as Balder or an Aryan—even when he is claimed to have origins near Goslar.

The Oriental desert doctrine declares: Woman is inferior, woman is sinful, woman is subordinate, woman is impure. To ensure that a woman thus characterized does not regain influence over family and community, she is also commanded to remain silent. Paul says:

"I do not permit a woman to teach or to assume authority over a man; she must be quiet,"

and further:

"A woman should learn in quietness and full submission."

And:

"Let your women keep silent in the churches, for they are not permitted to speak; but they are to be submissive, as the law also says."

With this, the influence of women on the family was undermined. How can a son respect the advice of a mother who does not even have the right to hold a political opinion? If he did so anyway, it was because his German blood contradicted the Jewish law. Thus, a son's attitude toward his mother has become a measure of his blood and soul.

This law deprived women of any influence on the affairs of the people.

Unfortunately, this attitude toward women persists even today. It is emphasized that women should stay out of politics. This means they are not to concern themselves with the affairs of the people. It is again said that women should be "maids and servants," or that women belong to the "**K**" words: children (*Kinder*), church (*Kirche*), kitchen (*Küche*), and clothes (*Kleider*).

This is synagogue thinking. The theologian Professor Reinhold Seeberg correctly states:

"Christian teaching, in its views on marriage and sexual life, has largely aligned itself with Judaism."

But we want to be Germans!

CHAPTER

4

THE GERMAN WOMAN IN THE MIDDLE AGES

The brutalization of societal customs, caused by the exclusion of women from influencing public affairs and the terrible vilification of their gender, is evident when comparing the Christian Middle Ages to the earlier "pagan" era.

When the Christianized 13th century composed the *Nibelungenlied* based on Germanic traditions, the poets had already become so de-Germanized that they depicted Siegfried as a husband who beat his wife:

"Siegfried has bruised my body,"

and considered such behavior compatible with Germanic heroism. They also had Krimhild and Brunhild, the proud Valkyrie, enter the church—to pray!

Of course, German children today are not to know that a Krimhild and a Brunhild never prayed, yet were so filled with pride in God and illuminated by divine spirit. Germanic sources were thus obscured, placing at the forefront of the heroic sagas the repugnant story of the dark elf Wieland and his vile, ignoble deeds against playing children and the enemy's daughter.

Even in the deepest misfortune, Germanic honor shielded heroes from such shameful revenge.

Among the Germanic people, it was considered disgraceful for a man to strike his wife. If he did, she separated from him or avenged the blow, and the community approved of such actions.

King Olaf demanded that Sigrid, his bride, be baptized and become a Christian. But she said:

"I will never abandon my old faith. Nor will I argue with you if you choose to believe in the god that pleases you."

At this, King Olaf, full of anger, exclaimed:

"How could I marry you, you heathen dog!"

and struck her in the face with his glove before rising to leave. King Olaf was a Christian. Sigrid said:

"This will bring about your death someday."

Sigrid married the King of Denmark, who avenged her against Olaf. In a sea battle, Olaf was defeated and met his death in the ocean. Thus did the Germanic woman repay such an insult. Public opinion sided with her, and she was vindicated.

Compare this with the Middle Ages, with its crude farces and carnival plays in the time of Hans Sachs. During this period, it was considered a source of public amusement when husbands "tamed" their wives with beatings. A man who did not strike his wife was mocked as a "henpecked husband," while one who was particularly brutal was praised as a "manly" spouse. And the degenerate, morally corrupt populace laughed at this, calling such brutality a joke.

The Greek Orthodox Church, even into the 17th century, demanded the abuse of women. The *Domostroy*, a moral-religious guidebook issued by Bishop Sylvester during this time, instructed men that it was their "moral duty" to discipline their wives and children with a whip.

In 14th-century Breslau, a husband accused of brutality had to promise to punish his wife only with rods *"as is proper and fitting for an honorable man, according to faith and conscience."*

A Passau law book from the same century stated:

"What a man has to do with his housewife is not subject to worldly courts, only to spiritual penance."

In old Bavarian law, it was written:

"The right to discipline, both in words and deeds, is also an extension of the husband's authority."

This perspective is upheld by the Church even today. The Church's marriage regulations, as outlined in *"The Marriage of the Christian"* state:

"Her husband's decisions and orders are her guiding principles. Her husband is the head who leads and governs. She follows and obeys. She is a daughter of Sarah, as she calls her husband 'Lord.'"

A fine comparison for a German woman: Sarah, the Jewess, who was bartered by her husband, the patriarch Abraham, to foreign kings.

If the German woman truly wishes to remain under synagogue law, then she must also endure without complaint what *"The Marriage of the Christian"* further demands of her as a "daughter of Sarah" (ibid, p. 35ff):

"Or her husband may take pleasure in provoking and tormenting her, perhaps even abusing her—how great the danger then for her to repay him in kind instead of humbling herself even more deeply. She has given herself to him and keeps her place in humility, for she knows that she belongs to him and will remain his as long as he lives."

And what does the Civil Code say? It grants the right to divorce only in cases of "severe" mistreatment (§ 1568). Where the boundary lies between so-called *"severe"* and *"mild"* mistreatment is left to the discretion of a male judge.

Germanic law did not recognize a church blessing for marriage. In pre-Christian times, the father or guardian of the bride united the couple with the Germanic greeting, the arm raised high and armed with a sword. A few but deeply felt words made a sermon unnecessary:

"Keep your home sacred."

The bridal adornment, which makes the church blessing seem indispensable to many, is just as much an ancient Germanic custom as the pagan Polterabend (wedding-eve celebration), which is still joyfully celebrated without a priest. Even written Germanic law considered the priest unnecessary for marriage.

Charlemagne (the Cruel), who brought so much misfortune to German lands, decreed in his capitularies of 802 (Chapter 35) that marriage could only be solemnized by clergy and secular authorities under a church blessing. Yet Charlemagne himself, the pious reformer, had only seven wives, and his daughters lived in free unions. He was thus a faithful student of the "wise" Solomon. His decree did not take hold.

As late as 1291, Archbishop Konrad of Salzburg had to concede that the Church would be content if only the marriage were reported to the pastor within a month of its conclusion. Gradually, however, the Church succeeded in replacing the guardian with the priest, and legal marriage began to take place before the church doors and in the presence of a priest.

Instead of a guardian who protected her, the woman was now given a confessor. The spiritual bond between husband and wife was destroyed by the confessional, and the privacy and sanctity of marriage were taken away. What questions the priest is allowed to ask, and how women are taught hypocrisy and falsehood toward their husbands, is detailed in Dr. Mathilde Ludendorff's booklet, "*A Glimpse into the Moral Teachings of the Roman Church.*"

A Germanic marriage could be dissolved with mutual consent and without difficulty. Each spouse took their property and was free again. If the marriage had been entered into before witnesses, it was dissolved before witnesses as well. If aversion, mistreatment, adultery, or attempted murder occurred, the written Germanic law dissolved the marriage.

The Church, however, made marriage a sacrament and declared it indissoluble in the 11th century.

"*Marriages are made in heaven,*"

blind believers claim, without considering that this statement reduces God to an undoubtedly very clumsy matchmaker and holds Him responsible for all the suffering caused by unhappy unions.

Adultery did not dissolve a marriage. The Church alone decided on its validity and continuation, but not based on reasons of purity or morality. In Bavaria, the Church even imposed penalties for separation if it was carried out due to aversion. Divorced individuals were not allowed to remarry. Different principles, however, applied to nobility and political figures.

The free-spirited and joyful interactions between the sexes, customary among the ancestors, came to an end. Joint bathing was prohibited as early as 745 by Boniface. The *Fechtspiegel* and *Bußordnungen* (penitential laws) declared it a sin. Washing as little as possible was considered especially pleasing to God.

The Germanic people cherished both external and internal cleanliness, physical hardening, and activity in the fresh air, believing in a healthy mind within a healthy, well-conditioned body. The Middle Ages despised and opposed all forms of physical culture. One of Saint Elisabeth's most notable virtues was said to be that she never washed, which supposedly greatly increased her sanctity.

A body deprived of air and water naturally weakened and degenerated. The restrictive clothing of the time, which prevented the body from breathing, further contributed to this decline. A once vigorous, weather-hardened people became a nation of frail, weakened indoor dwellers. With physical decay came moral and spiritual decline.

The purity of social interactions between men and women was lost. At festivals, men and women now sat separately. The housewife relinquished her place of honor to the priest, sitting to her husband's left while the priest took the seat of honor on his right.

Instead of joyful folk songs and dances, which the Church banned, festivals began with masses, and hymns were sung. Women's beauty was veiled in the Oriental fashion, revealing only the eyes, nose, and mouth. Ulrich von Lichtenstein wrote in his *Frauenbuch* (1257):

"*Like nuns, women now cover their cheeks, mouths, and foreheads with veils and bands, leaving only their eyes visible. And if one dresses in a worldly and cheerful manner, she at least wears a rosary as a brooch, so that men are constantly reminded of piety.*"

Preachers of the Middle Ages painted a grim picture of women's indifference in church:

"*The church is used as a place for gossip and for seeing and being seen.*"

This proves how the foreign doctrine led to hypocrisy because it did not take root in the German soul. It was not a natural, soul-born piety but a contrived devoutness shaped by foreign ideals. Is it any wonder, then, that many women degenerated under its influence, becoming deceitful and hypocritical? They could only live up to these foreign models by abandoning their own nature.

Men adopted the Jewish view of women and could no longer think purely or nobly of friendship between the sexes. Many women, in turn, adopted the Oriental desert ideal to which they were reduced. They sold themselves like Sarah, deceived like Rebecca, seduced like Judith and Esther, though none ever reached the perversity of a Delilah or a Salome.

"German women, German loyalty," still proclaims the German national anthem today. Gudrun still lives, despite a thousand years of captivity! How healthy and pure must the German woman's soul have been to withstand this estrangement and poisoning for so long. Even Walther von der Vogelweide sang, at the end of the 12th century:

"They are better here than the women of other lands"

and

"German women are angelic and pure; foolish is anyone who could insult them. Virtue and true love—whoever seeks them should come to our land, for here love abounds."

Of course, the courtly love of the Middle Ages, with its sweet sentimentality—so exaggerated that knights would drink the washwater of their beloveds—had nothing in common with Germanic respect and honor for women. It was of Romance origin. Thus, it did not take root in Scandinavian countries, which remained more untouched by such influences.

Rather than deepening marriage, courtly love undermined it. Chivalry stopped at the husband's own doorstep and wife, dedicating itself instead to the wives of others. Knights pursued "the lady of their hearts," wearing her colors in tournaments, fighting for her, showering her with love gifts, and even embarking on crusades to absolve themselves of guilt.

This sense of guilt led husbands to treat their wives like harem women, supervised by an overseer, a *"Merker."* The poet Ulrich von Lichtenstein, who went so far as to present his beloved with his severed finger as a token of devotion, records in his Frauenbuch (1257) a dialogue between a knight and a lady about the decay of society.

The knight accuses women of being responsible for men withdrawing and becoming wild because women reject them, barely return their greetings, and respond sparingly to questions. As a result, men turn elsewhere for entertainment.

The lady replies that women cannot be friendly and open because they know such behavior will be misinterpreted, leading to the loss of their honor. Gone are the days when the hostess could greet a guest with a friendly smile and kiss and join in the dance. Spontaneous cheerfulness is now falsely interpreted, so women have abandoned it.

"How neglected some wives are! All day long, their husbands are out hunting, returning late, throwing themselves at the table, and demanding a board game."

When not hunting, men sit drinking wine, boasting and gossiping about their conquests with women, cutting away their honor.

"Each man brags about what happened with one woman or another. This was not so before. Those who earned a woman's love once knew how to keep silent about it."

The knight raises further accusations. He claims that the loss of pure love is the fault of women who sell themselves for gifts or even money.

The lady counters with a severe accusation against noblemen, saying that a virtuous woman cannot be good enough for them because everyone knows what unnatural vices flourish among them.

"There are still plenty of pure and chaste women, but men do not know how to value such pearls."

To this, the knight has no reply.

A look back into the Germanic past reveals the devastating effects of Roman influence, unnatural asceticism, and celibacy. The men became brutalized and morally degenerate, while the women sank into either excessive piety, licentiousness, or both. All poets of the 14th and 15th centuries who viewed their time with seriousness rendered the same judgment. They consistently contrasted the present unfavorably with the past.

The Austrian poet Teichner (14th century) lamented that money was now the sole ruler, a man's word held no value, faith was in decline, and violence, murder, and lies had gained the upper hand. Similarly, Walther von der Vogelweide expressed similar grievances at the end of his life.

It is clear that this decline was caused by the foreign faith, the uprooting of people from their soul-born and innate spiritual worldview, and the associated degradation and desecration of the love life. This decline cannot simply be reversed by reforming swimwear. The laments of poets in France and Germany show that this deterioration began to manifest as early as the 12th century.

Heinrich von Rucke (12th century) lamented that Jews and Christians thought only of making money, that women—though still virtuous, save for a few exceptions—were increasingly undervalued, as loyalty and honor meant little in a world consumed by greed. Men who gained the favor of noble women betrayed their trust by discarding discretion and boasting of their conquests.

The treatment of women and the behavior of men toward them reflects the moral level of a people. Though the Germanic tribes may have seemed rough and harsh, they nevertheless honored and respected their women, ensuring order and decency.

Germanic women could travel freely and without harassment—on horseback, by carriage, or even across the sea. However, in the subsequent Christian era, women faced unwanted advances and slander for such independence. Princes and clergy, meanwhile, traveled to imperial diets and councils accompanied by harems rivaling that of King Solomon. For example, the Basel and Constance councils each included 1,500 "traveling ladies."

Germanic morality did not tolerate prostitution, as Roman reports from the 4th and 5th centuries attest. Bishop Silvianus wrote that the Vandals imposed the death penalty for public indecency. The northern Germanic tribes, which retained their native faith and racial purity for longer, also upheld their famed moral integrity. The Saxons, Frisians, and Icelanders were distinguished for this, as reflected in their penal codes. Boniface reported that the Saxons forced a dishonored girl to take her own life, and her seducer was likewise executed.

In contrast, the Christian state made prostitution a state-protected trade, and the Church officially tolerated concubinage until the Lateran Council of 1511.

In earlier times, Germanic girls participated in the education of their era. Later, education became the exclusive privilege of noblewomen and nuns, while for others, the Psalter was deemed sufficient.

Frankfurt
Women in the Middle Ages
(*From German Folk Costumes by Friedrich Hottenroth*)

Nuremberg
Women in the Middle Ages
(*From German Folk Costumes by Friedrich Hottenroth*)

It became the women's book of instruction. Schools were few, and they were under the control of monasteries. Thus, women fell further into ignorance and superficiality, leading to intellectual subjugation to men, from which most have not yet freed themselves and, according to church doctrine, are not even supposed to.

Centuries of devaluation stunted their creative potential and stripped them of self-confidence. Where could they have regained it, when they were so disrespected, and church fathers, revered as representatives of God by all the "pious," were permitted to heap such scorn upon them?

Tertullian declared: *"Woman, you should always go in mourning and rags, your eyes full of tears of repentance, to erase the memory of your destruction of the human race. Woman, you are the gateway to hell. Celibacy must be chosen, even if the human race perishes."*

Origen stated: *"Marriage is something unholy and impure."*

Augustine proclaimed: *"The celibate will shine in heaven like radiant stars, while their parents will resemble dim ones."*

Anselm, Archbishop of Canterbury, declared: *"Flee, holy man, from the company of women. All fires of passion are ignited by women. If you could see into them, you would perceive the filth concealed beneath their white skin. O shepherds, keep the she-wolves away from your flocks; women are the death of the soul."*

The only way for girls to retain a sense of self-respect was to enter a convent, where they might possibly redeem their inherent sinfulness through a halo of sanctity. As nuns, they were allowed to receive an education, and their ecstatic visions were praised because they were inspired by the theological training of their confessors. These outpourings were carefully preserved, and the nuns were canonized. Saint Hildegard (1179) could "miraculously" recite the entire Bible from memory.

These physically and spiritually entombed, artificially weakened beings babbled about angels and demons, saints and martyrs, and irrational miracles. They experienced states of supernatural rapture that were alien to the Germanic woman and had nothing in common with her prophetic visions.

The Germanic pagan seeress, when she looked into the future, foretold the destiny of her people based on natural laws, her connection to nature, and her deep roots in the past. These ties gave her a vision of the future of the universe and the divinely established order, much like how the philosopher of the soul, Dr.

Mathilde Ludendorff, proclaims in her works.

Christian seeresses, however, directed their focus heavenward, glorifying unnatural miracles. Their souls no longer belonged to their people but longed for personal, otherworldly experiences of heavenly bliss or an afterlife that defied natural laws.

A remembrance of the once-heroic era still slumbered in the subconscious of the Christian German woman. It resurfaces even today, reborn in every German child as their sacred racial heritage, as long as the blood remains somewhat pure. Thus, the woman of the Middle Ages wove the ancient Germanic heroic sagas into tapestries and wall hangings. She depicted Sigmund's richly carved and gilded ships setting sail or Siegfried slaying the dragon. The buried knowledge of past greatness was passed on in the women's quarters. There, she told children the sagas and fairy tales in which our ancestors, during the final moments of their indigenous faith, had encapsulated the serious fate of their people.

At that time, they preserved these stories from the encroachments of the Church, whispering them secretly in their attics—stories of the German Snow White and her wicked stepmother behind the seven mountains (a metaphor for the city of seven hills) that suffocated and poisoned the German soul, reducing it to a death-like paralysis, entombing it as it awaited its revival. Or of Sleeping Beauty, who, poisoned by foreign influences, falls into a deep slumber and is encased by thorns (representing lies and falsehoods) until a great figure of her people clears the path of truth, tears apart the web of deceit, and liberates the German soul.

To suppress the experiences awakened by such stories, women were forbidden in the confessional to utter "magic spells" while weaving and spinning.

Even the Germanic names, whose sounds evoked heroic pride, had to disappear. Instead of Sigrun, Krimhild, Gudrun, Sunnihilt (the sun-like), Mathild (the powerful fighter), Gerhilt, or Gunhilt, there came Katharina, Maria, Anna, Josephine, Christine, Rebekka, Esther, and so on—just as among men, names like Christian, Jakob, David, and others took their place. Today, the Church again pushes for only Christian names to be chosen. They fear the Germanic heroic spiritual heritage and its reawakening.

"*The talisman* (the Christian doctrine, ed.) *is rotten, and the day will come when it collapses miserably,*" lamented the Jew Heine in anxious forewarning.

The Reformation did not bring significant improvement to the German woman's estimation or position. It could not, as it still rested on Christian doctrine. While monasteries were dissolved, the Protestant clergy freed from the obligation of celibacy, and German family life thereby given greater value, the woman's right to her husband's fidelity was restored. This principle, admittedly, also exists in the Catholic Church, but it becomes nullified through confession, penance, and indulgence. Women were freed from the confessor, and marriage regained its chaste exclusivity.

Although the Church priest was happily excluded or at least restricted in his rights, the husband remained, in essence, the house priest. For Luther also maintained: *"Had Eve not sinned, she would have ruled and governed alongside Adam as his helper. But now, authority belongs to him, and she must bow before him as her lord."*

While Luther later completely rejected the Old Testament and wrote, *"What do I care about Moses with his Ten Commandments? Go to the Jews with your Moses,"* he nevertheless adhered, as a Christian, to the Oriental view that sensual life is impure and abstinence holy. Under the influence of the Jew Paul, he regarded marriage as *"a remedy against sin, a hospital for the sick, so that they do not fall into greater sins."*

Luther, like most Germans, perhaps did not realize that this reduced the wife to a state-approved concubine of her husband. The Oriental knows no spiritual union between man and woman. To him, the woman is a commodity, property he acquires like any other, and in his homeland, depending on his wealth, he could have as many as he desired in his harem. For values not traded on the market, the Jew has no comprehension. One cannot reproach him for this—it is his inherent nature. However, a German should not adopt Jewish thinking and Jewish valuation of women.

It demeans German men when they say, "The blonde woman is highly valued in today's market."

CHAPTER

5

THE LONGING FOR FREEDOM OF THE GERMAN WOMAN

Throughout the Middle Ages, the German woman endured profound intellectual and physical subjugation to men. The Church rightly feared that the awakening of the Germanic woman posed its greatest threat. Hence, the horrific, centuries-long witch persecutions. These persecutions targeted the blonde women of Nordic-influenced lands; it was primarily here that the Church sought its victims, aiming for their systematic eradication. Predominantly young girls, women, and mothers were burned.

"A torrent of witches flooded northern Germany under Lutheranism," wrote a prominent Jesuit, "such that in some places, few women remain." The papal inquisitors Heinrich Institoris and Jakob Sprenger authored the Malleus Maleficarum (*The Hammer of Witches*), which served as the legal framework for the diabolical torment, torture, and burning that continued until the end of the 18th century. This text proclaimed:

"If we investigate, we will find that almost all the kingdoms of the world have perished because of women. Were it not for the wickedness of women, the world would be free from countless dangers."

In churches, denunciation boxes were installed, allowing anyone to submit accusations at will. Little effort was made to discern whether the allegations were malicious slander or grounded in truth; the torture chamber would determine that.

And with what heroism was all of this endured! Many women faced death rather than bow to the priest or confess guilt for crimes of which their souls were innocent. They allowed their limbs to be torn from their joints, walked over glowing iron plates, were pierced with nails, buried alive, or burned at a slow fire—enduring it all without recanting.

With a cold, murderous hand, Rome crushed the flowers of our people and trampled them underfoot. If a woman distinguished herself particularly, she might later be canonized, as was Jeanne d'Arc (Joan of Arc), the heroic maiden of Orléans who liberated her French people only to be burned at the stake in gratitude—for the crime of "wearing men's clothing."

Rome understood that as long as Nordic blood pulsed within the peoples, its goals remained unattainable. Thus, it sought to eradicate this blood through crusades, pyres, wars, and, not least, racial mixing. The Germanic peoples had long adhered to the principle of marrying only within their tribe. Marriages with Romans were invalid. The Christian doctrine of indiscriminate love among humans led to the erosion of these sacred principles of racial purity. Nonetheless, German marital laws continued to make intermarriage with Jews rare until the 18th century. A healthy, blood-bound rejection persisted despite the teaching of this people's supposed "chosenness."

The Jew, however, masterfully concealed his distinct ethnic identity under the guise of religious opposition to Christianity, presenting himself as merely a "different believer." Even our greatest Germans were deceived by this ruse, leading to the disastrous tolerance of Frederick the Great toward the Jews and inspiring Lessing's Nathan the Wise, which served Jewish interests.

This stance by political and intellectual leaders, the opening of the ghettos, and especially the French Revolution—with its Jewish-promoted slogans of liberty, equality, and fraternity—tore down all barriers and led to indiscriminate racial intermingling. This was a great victory for the Jew, granting him social acceptability. While princes had long favored him as a financier, they had maintained a distance. The nobility, increasingly dependent on him, now offered him their blonde daughters—a triumphant moment for Ahasverus (the Wandering Jew) and a disgrace for the German aristocracy. Following the nobility's lead, the bourgeoisie also succumbed, leaving the working class as the last bastion of healthy instincts.

The consequences soon became apparent. The blood of a cowardly, fear-stricken, mercantile desert people brought decay and ruin to the heroic spirit and noble character of the North. The aristocracy, which had once fought Frederick the Great's battles and distinguished itself during the wars of liberation, gradually withdrew from later conflicts, and the bourgeoisie degenerated into a materialistic, petty middle class.

Many robust Nordic peoples have perished through intermarriage with the Orient. The healthier and more heroic they were, the longer they managed to resist. Racial purity is as essential to the survival of a people as it is to any species of plant or animal. They only crossbreed with equals, with those of the same kind. German children are thoroughly taught to differentiate between cruciferous plants, labiates, or composites, yet they learn little about the differences between human races and nothing about their unique spiritual qualities.

In the direst moments of racial decline, some peoples recognized the significance of blood—a truth the Jew has preserved through the centuries. In England, he was an Englishman; in France, a Frenchman; in Germany, an internationalist or sometimes a nationalist German. Yet everywhere, he remained a Jew, conscious of his blood. His people were always his highest value. Without this, he would have assimilated into other nations long ago. He understood that indiscriminate racial mixing leads to the death of a people.

And we know today that the diversity of nations is divinely ordained, and that nations have the right to freely develop their God-given uniqueness, just as every living being in nature may do. To infringe upon this right is sacrilege. The ethnic awakening of our time gives hope that we will return to ourselves—not through the "breeding" of Nordic people, but through the voluntary selection based on spiritual and intellectual kinship, guided by the ideal of Nordic beauty. Led by these ideas, the German people could, within a few generations, resemble the original image of their ancestors. This is affirmed by Mendel's laws of inheritance.

For the spider-like entity of Rome-Judah, such an awakened, self-reclaimed "Siegfried nation" would indeed be a devastating defeat. Hence, its deliberate striving toward a European world conflagration, which would turn defenseless Germany into a theater of war, paving the way for the desired mixture of peoples and the "Eurasian-Negroid race." Self-aware nations, after all, cannot be enslaved.

The Nordic woman has fought for her freedom, her participation in education, and her influence on national affairs throughout the centuries. In this struggle, she has always faced the fiercest resistance. When individual women were granted influence over political matters, it was often those who—like an Esther—used their eroticism to influence statesmen and leaders, often bringing great calamity to their nations. This bitterly avenged the fact that women were valued only for their sexuality, while noble, pure women who despised such means were forced into silence.

Nevertheless, some women distinguished themselves for the benefit of their nations, demonstrating strength and foresight. For example, Elizabeth of England or Maria Theresa. Although the latter was swayed by her confessor to wage war against Frederick the Great, when her entire confessional record—entrusted to her Jesuit confessor—was sent to her from Madrid, she banned the Jesuit order in Austria. She also put an end to witch trials in her country and opposed Freemasonry.

The prevailing rejection of politically active women often relegated them to subordinate roles. Maria Theresa, for instance, was formally co-regent with her son, though behind them stood the nefarious influence of Kaunitz, who constrained her as well as Queen Louise. Despite Louise's pleas and warnings, she could not convince her husband, the weak Frederick William III, to free himself from the clutches of Freemasonry. Queen Louise clearly recognized its pernicious influence on the king. She knew that only the spirit of a Friedrich Schiller could save Prussia and sought to bring him to Berlin. His death "at the right time" thwarted her plan. Schiller might have prevented the disaster at Jena.

Both princesses, who combined abundant maternal instincts with political acumen, recognized secret orders as a threat to the state. Had they fully understood the customs and oaths of Freemasonry, they would likely have condemned the lodges as immoral as well. If German women married to Freemasons knew about the degrading rituals their husbands participated in within these lodges, including their binding oaths to "blind obedience" to further a global agenda, they would likely be the swift demise of this secretive institution.

Women, driven by their maternal instincts, would oppose the subjugation of their children to slavery, expropriation, unpaid labor, and ultimately to wars waged not for national freedom but for the benefit of global financial elites. Did any nation truly emerge victorious from the last World War? *"The Pope was the only winner,"* noted the Roman press during the unveiling of the monument to Benedict XV, the so-called *"War Pope."*

To prevent women from awakening to these realities, efforts were made to keep them politically ignorant and uncritical, steering them toward superficialities and distractions, making them apathetic and detached. Men, too, would never have been drawn into secret societies so extensively had they not been conditioned from an early age to devalue women, ensuring they later sought "refinement" not at home but in the lodges. Once stripped of their dignity and self-respect through the absurdities they engaged in there, they were more inclined to adopt demeaning views of women as a way to justify themselves to both their wives and themselves.

The subjugated man, trained in blind obedience, was compensated by being allowed to dominate his wife. Just as the Bible includes the commandment *"Thou shalt not covet thy neighbor's wife"*—with "neighbor" in this context referring only to fellow tribesmen—Freemasonry also requires an oath not to seduce a fellow brother's wife. How this expanded sense of morality affects the behavior of some members raises questions. Such oaths aim to bind members firmly to the order. The more morally compromised a man becomes, the more unscrupulous and thus more suitable he is for the crimes demanded by these secret societies. Conversely, the purer the woman he finds at home—untainted by these influences—the more likely he is to attempt to dominate her. Her integrity stands as a constant reproach to his depravity.

It was well understood that the majority of women would not participate in the crimes committed against the people by secret orders. Even the initiation rituals of Freemasonry would evoke healthy disgust in women, rooted in their natural sense of cleanliness and aesthetic sensibility. Women would also reject the secrecy imposed on family members.

During the Freemason-led revolution of 1789, French women demanded the right to speak from the tribune if they were to be sent to the scaffold. They opposed the execution of the king, revolted against the reign of terror, and saw the heroic Charlotte Corday assassinate the beast Marat. In response, all women's political associations were dissolved "for public safety and the nature of women." The revolutionary slogan *"rights of man"* did not apply to women, as "man" and "human" were treated as synonymous. The few voices that insisted women were also human beings and deserved the "eternal rights of humanity" were silenced. Women were initially incited to participate in the overthrow of the old order, but only so their support could be exploited to secure power. As soon as they sought to exert influence, the principle of physical strength prevailed. While "might over right" is generally condemned as immoral, it has always been applied to women.

The Enlightenment of the 18th and 19th centuries marked a widespread rejection of the Bible, driven by scientific discoveries about the universe and the evolution of life. These discoveries completely discredited the biblical creation myth. Friedrich the Great's attitude toward Christianity, which he dismissed as *"Oriental fantasy,"* his advocacy for freedom of conscience and religious tolerance, the ethical liberty taught by German idealism (especially associated with Schiller), and Kant's philosophy of moral autonomy based on self-determined inner law—all these movements loosened the chains binding German women. They promoted moral equality between the sexes and acknowledged women's right to self-determination and personal development.

The liberation from the Bible also meant freedom from Christianity's denigration of the body. Wigs disappeared. Friedrich Jahn inspired German youth to embrace physical fitness and resilience. Women's clothing began to reflect this liberation, highlighting the natural beauty of the body. However, under the rigidly pious Friedrich Wilhelm IV, these freedoms regressed, and restrictive hoop skirts reappeared.

The principle of male dominance was now upheld only insofar as love and respect justified it. *"The husband must always appear to her as the most honorable and respectable of all,"* taught Fichte. Thus, voluntary submission without coercion arose from the harmony of feelings and will. Otherwise, couples could not be expected to remain together. Fichte stated: *"Spouses separate of their own free will, just as they joined together. If they agree on the terms of the separation, they merely need to notify the state of their decision. Only in cases of dispute should the state assist, and even then, the state should facilitate divorce, particularly when requested unilaterally—especially by the wife—because without love, she cannot be forced to continue the marriage."*

The demand for freedom of conscience also brought the struggle against ecclesiastical jurisdiction in marital matters and against church-sanctioned weddings. Bismarck's major reform—the law allowing withdrawal from the church and the introduction of civil marriage in 1873—advanced the German woman's fight for freedom, which she had always waged, albeit often unconsciously.

She deeply felt her chains but did not always know where they were anchored. Freedom of conscience, the mother of "human rights," also became the creator of women's rights.

However, just as the workers' struggle for freedom was co-opted and distorted by Jewish influence into a class struggle, so too was the German woman's will for freedom. The Jews recognized the enormous threat posed by this drive for freedom—both from workers and women—and sought to redirect it into channels that protected their own interests while outwardly accommodating the spirit of the times. The Jewish woman Goldschmidt became the leader of the General German Women's Association, originally founded on October 18, 1865— Leipzig's victory day—by the German-born Luise Otto-Peters. What began as an idealistic struggle for freedom turned into a fight for wages and competition.

The Nordic woman had not sought equality out of economic necessity but rather out of a desire for freedom and human dignity rooted in her racial heritage. Many even embraced this cause at the cost of leaving lives of wealth and comfort for economic uncertainty and hardship. This spirit was continually revived by German women, such as Käthe Schirmacher, who famously said, *"Honor's essence is that one dies for it."*

However, Jewish influence in leadership (e.g., Leite, Morgenstern, Anita Augspurg) ensured that the right to work took precedence, pushing women into competition with men. Instead of fostering the natural unity and complementarity between the sexes, a new divide was created. The right to work—as though the German woman, in the majority, had not always worked—became the central issue.

Jewish global capitalism quickly seized upon women's willingness to work and earn, exploiting their labor in factories. Women, accustomed to working under conditions of subordination and without wages, became prime targets for industrial exploitation, providing the greatest profits for large-scale industry.

The slogan "A woman's place is in the home" was conveniently ignored here. Young women, without regard for their physical development or training for their future roles as housewives and mothers, were confined to factory spaces. Later, the lack of preparation for domestic and educational responsibilities often led to unhappy marriages, neglected children, disorderly households, and poorly cooked meals, all of which undermined even the happiest of unions.

The German male-dominated state took no consideration for the wife or her domestic role. Women were exploited without hesitation, even pregnant mothers were not spared. The argument of the *"weaker sex,"* otherwise so frequently invoked, was conveniently ignored here. Women were expected to manage two professions and serve two masters, even at the expense of their health, maternal duties, and the well-being of their children and home. The physical and emotional toll on overburdened women was disregarded.

In contrast, theologians and others often raised concerns about women engaging in scholarly pursuits, claiming it could harm their ability to fulfill their maternal responsibilities. Yet, it has been proven that intellectual work does not negatively affect motherhood. Heinrich von Treitschke once proclaimed, *"Because we thought too narrowly to grant women the freedom of education, only a minority of German women today are capable of understanding the serious demands of our times."* However, when a woman did pursue studies, she was often ridiculed, even by her peers, as a *"bluestocking."* If she achieved something noteworthy or merely earned a doctorate, it was regarded as an extraordinary feat—failing to recognize how this perspective undervalued her sacred role as a mother.

The women's movement was initially limited to founding public kitchens, sewing schools, nurseries, kindergartens, and similar initiatives. It was not until 1908 that university education was formally opened to German women. After 38 years of effort, the bourgeois women's movement finally achieved a reform of girls' schools, allowing women to take final examinations. Prior to this, women aspiring to study had to prepare through real-school or gymnasium courses and were admitted and examined at only a few universities. Käthe Schumacher, for example, had to study in France and earn her doctorate in Switzerland because the Christian-conservative spirit still dominated, particularly in the so-called upper class. Meanwhile, the working class, with its more natural and progressive outlook, often treated women with far greater equality.

Even the otherwise nationally-minded Paul de Lagarde declared in 1884, as part of the conservative party's platform on women's issues: *"The girl, even one from higher social classes, should learn what everyone must know today: reading, writing, arithmetic, and some local geography. Beyond that, what she learns, apart from sewing, knitting, and cooking as taught by her mother, depends solely on the life God has assigned her. Every woman truly learns only from the man she loves, and she learns whatever and as much as he desires and values through his love. It is proper for girls to marry and gain their education within marriage. Sisters, daughters, and caregivers will also be shaped by brothers, fathers, the sick, and the elderly, as they serve men with warm hearts."*

This stance reflects a deeply troubling blindness born of male vanity and selfishness—a result of centuries of Christian indoctrination. It marks a sad deviation from the more balanced and honorable view of women in Germanic thought and tradition.

The will for freedom of the German woman increasingly defied all resistance. To channel this will away from the proper path of participating in public affairs, a new outlet was repeatedly provided: access to sports. Previously deemed inappropriate for women, and once limited by strict boundaries, women were now encouraged to engage in sports activities. However, many of these activities often severely harmed their bodies, rendering them unfit for motherhood. It was particularly the healthiest and most agile women who were thus excluded from contributing to the growth of the population.

Sports became a societal epidemic, striving for records that led to overstrained nerves and heart issues, and ultimately had little in common with genuine physical fitness. The Nordic individual, with their natural love for physical agility, was so captivated by this enthusiasm that they lost focus on themselves and the world around them. In this state of distraction, they ceased to pose any obstacle to the plans of certain elements exploiting nations for their gain. The German people were effectively kept as short-sighted "dayflies," detached from their past, fixated only on daily events. Meanwhile, others, thinking in centuries, pursued far-reaching goals with cold calculation.

These dynamics allowed for the rapid creation of magnificent sports facilities without financial constraints, while resources for healthy housing—vital to fostering happy family life and the strength of the nation—were severely neglected or overlooked entirely.

In women's sports, the same mistake was made as in education and professional endeavors. The fundamental differences between the genders were ignored, as Dr. Ludendorff highlighted in her book *Das Weib und seine Bestimmung* (The Woman and Her Purpose). When women struggled in areas that were intrinsically aligned with masculine domains, this was misconstrued as evidence of the inferiority of women. This dogma persisted stubbornly, as many men found it far too difficult to relinquish their notion of superiority and instead respect women as equal yet fundamentally different in nature.

CHAPTER

6

THE DISTINCT NATURE OF MAN & WOMAN & ITS IMPORTANCE FOR FAMILY & NATION

The achievements credited to the women's movement so far have only brought partial or superficial success to women. What use was the right to vote, which gave women the illusion of equality? They did not secure a proportionate number of female representatives corresponding to their voter base. Instead, they elected men who then, without the inclusion of women but with their electoral power, built a one-sided male-dominated state. Such a system, being contrary to divine natural laws, cannot foster true restoration.

Dr. Käthe Schirmacher, a brave pioneer, rightly stated:

"The perception of women as an inferior, functionally subordinate gender is completely un-Germanic, and it is astonishing to encounter this view, especially in

völkisch circles that claim to abhor all things Jewish-Oriental. Here, this mentality clings tightly to their consciousness. Can the völkisch spirit of women renew Germany? Would this renewal come from a subjugated, subordinate female and maternal gender? What often keeps conservative and national women distant from the German women's movement is the belief that it is un-Germanic and foreign to their heritage. In truth, the women's movement, which only sprouted and bore useful fruits in Germanic lands, seeks to reclaim for Germanic women their ancient heritage. The Germanic woman was both militant and domestic, and for these dual attributes, she was highly respected. She was strong and fought alongside men in battle, sometimes falling alongside them. She found joy in combat, as evidenced by the valkyries who stood beside the mother goddess Frigga. It is to this strong, pure, and striving womanhood that our path leads. The German male-dominated state fell apart in autumn 1918. The völkisch state, if it can ever be established, can only be realized through the collaboration of all social strata and both genders."

Nationalists recognize Käthe Schirmacher as one of their staunchest advocates. Yet, they disregard her stance on the women's question entirely. While they grant women the right to pursue professional work, they deny them influence over national affairs. Indeed, some go so far as to declare: *"Women are created solely for breeding and raising children."* Such synagogue-inspired attitudes in the nationalist camp reveal the moral quagmire into which Jewish sexual ethics have led men, reducing their view of women to that of the basest perspective.

Nature has created the world as dual-gendered, intending it to be governed by both genders in harmony. Nature desires gender differences and rejects any form of forced *"uniformity."* The effeminate man and the mannish woman are unnatural and thus repellent.

In her work *"The Woman and Her Purpose,"* Dr. Mathilde Ludendorff, as a specialist, explores the physical and psychological differences between men and women. For the first time, this research offers a comprehensive and objective study on the complementary abilities of the sexes. It puts an end to the simplistic and false dichotomy that "man is reason, woman is emotion," exposing the harm caused by male-dominated and female-dominated societies alike.

Dr. Ludendorff further demonstrates in her work *"The Healing of Love"* that the differences between the genders were established long before humanity existed—long before any question of male or female dominance could have arisen.

Books on the psychology of women written in earlier times often amounted to either flattering or disparaging lists of supposed female shortcomings. A man's judgment of women is inevitably influenced by his personal feelings—whether affection or antipathy—and shaped by his individual experiences. Thus, psychological evaluations of women provided by men have often failed under serious scrutiny.

Psychology is a relatively young science, perhaps because it does not align with the male inclination for different areas of study, given the varying directions of interest between genders. Only after women gained access to higher education were irrefutable and foundational insights achieved in this field. A German woman and mother, who also worked as a physician specializing in neurology and psychiatry, made significant breakthroughs. Dr. Mathilde Ludendorff, drawing from her philosophical, medical, and natural-scientific studies, as well as from the visionary intuition inherent to Germanic women, offered groundbreaking insights that herald a new era. Her work, *"The Woman and Her Purpose"*, presents a psychology of the sexes that has withstood scientific critique, though the internationally aligned academic establishment has deliberately ignored both her and her contributions. As long as theology—which often distances itself from truth—remains dominant within academic faculties, this neglect is unlikely to change.

Mathilde Ludendorff highlights the errors previously made in evaluating the physical and psychological traits of women. For example, it was often said that women have greater perceptive abilities, while men possess superior creative power, and these differences were ascribed to biological distinctions. Ludendorff rejects this as unscientific, pointing out that women contribute not only the germ cell but also the nurturing environment for its development, implying that women's creative mental capacities must be just as advanced as their perceptive abilities.

She demonstrates that the perceptive abilities of women are excellent in areas they find interesting and lackluster in those they find indifferent. Women excel in fields to which they voluntarily dedicate their attention. This characteristic is not exclusive to women but is common among emotionally robust individuals of any gender. Even highly gifted people can appear inept in areas that fail to capture their interest. However, women often receive less rigorous willpower training than men, who are more accustomed to being compelled by school, life, and professional obligations to focus on subjects they may find unappealing.

Conversely, women, being less accustomed to forcing their attention, often disengage from disinteresting topics, claiming they "don't understand" them. This behavior has led to the erroneous conclusion that women are intellectually inferior. Ludendorff aptly notes:

"This is simply a lack of discipline in training, which society tolerates in women because they are seldom reproached for lacking basic knowledge. On the contrary, such gaps are often excused as the so-called 'stupidity' of women. Some highly gifted women, for instance, claim they cannot understand a train schedule."

One can conclude that the areas to which women devote themselves with preference and passion are naturally women's domains, and these are more clearly delineated than men's domains, which, due to education and upbringing, are extended to include topics that might not personally resonate with men.

Because this reality was not previously understood, women were brought into professions that exclusively belonged to men. Their failure in such domains was then used to argue their intellectual inferiority. The question must instead be: On which areas or topics can women provide something more valuable than men?

Dr. Mathilde Ludendorff proves which areas reflect superior achievements by women and which are exclusively suited for men. In doing so, she dismantles the idea of the intellectual inferiority of women—a belief that gained many eager followers with the introduction of Jewish perspectives on women in Germany. She demonstrates that girls show better average results in memory and retention than boys. While memory was previously overvalued in education—given more importance than fostering critical thinking—memory and retention are nonetheless vital for true intellectual reasoning.

Another so-called "evidence" of women's intellectual inferiority is their perceived lack of logical thinking. Studies of boys and girls who received equal education reveal that girls solve mathematical problems just as well as boys. Since mathematics demands the most rigorous logical thinking, it follows that women also possess this ability. However, the stronger emotional life of women often interferes with their logical processes. Furthermore, their education has failed to cultivate this skill because logic has been dismissed as unimportant for them. Instead of fostering logical thinking in girls through proper schooling, this area has been neglected. The resulting claim that women lack logic is therefore a false conclusion.

In professions or sciences that do not engage women's emotional lives, their logical reasoning is just as strong as men's and is often enhanced by their unique capacity for intuition. Even critics of women admit to the superiority of this intuitive insight. This quality is also evident in emotionally rich men, and it has produced some of the most extraordinary achievements in art.

Despite this, there are comparatively fewer female creators of great works of art. The reason lies in the inherent psychological differences between men and women. Women, being more selfless and capable of greater sacrifice, often dedicate themselves entirely to an idea, just as they do to their love for others. This characteristic is also the foundation of their maternal instincts. Men, on the other hand, are naturally more self-serving, which is necessary for their survival. Emotional experiences serve as inspiration for men rather than consuming them entirely. This ensures that they can create without the same degree of internal distraction.

In many cases, women are denied the opportunity to express their creative potential because they are socially dependent—first on their parents and later on their husbands. This dependence limits their opportunities. Furthermore, women frequently face opposition from their social environments, which stand in stark contrast to their creative aspirations. Only women with a strong will for independence manage to overcome such restrictions, although not without great emotional hardship.

Only a few women, after centuries of education toward weakness and submissiveness, are capable of asserting their independence. For such a path demands a struggle both external and internal, and it is by no means guaranteed that this battle will end in victory for freedom and creative ability. Many idealists have been broken by the malice and vileness of their contemporaries. The shallow and complacent will always reject such struggles, shaking their heads in disbelief. A life of routine and inertia, surrounded by the most intellectually undemanding environment, satisfies them. Yet for the idealist, such a life is poison—leading either to consuming anguish or the death of the soul unless they break free.

The intellectual and economic dependence of women is undoubtedly a major cause of their lack of significant, groundbreaking creations. However, another equally serious reason lies in the centuries-long undervaluation of their intellectual capacities, which inevitably caused a profound lack of self-confidence. We know how poor paternal upbringing—one that denies freedom of intellectual development—can stifle even highly gifted sons, creating a lack of confidence in their own critical thinking and judgment. This can permanently inhibit their ability to create independently.

An artist must possess self-confidence in their work. They must feel an inner calling to create. Doubt in one's ability destroys creative power, just as spiteful criticism can extinguish the inspiration to create. Throughout the Christian centuries, women were consistently deprived of the self-confidence necessary for their endeavors. Women who produced excellent work often hid their creations under male pseudonyms to avoid the prejudice against female achievement.

This systematic devaluation of women's capabilities hindered their potential, creating a cycle of suppression that persists in subtle forms even today.

Even today, many girls grow up within families that perpetuate this devaluation of their intellectual abilities. A schoolboy may mock his sister's differing opinion with a dismissive Latin phrase, *"Mulier taceat in ecclesia"* (Let the woman keep silent in the church). Similarly, many women still echo sentiments like Dorothea's: *"I enjoy listening to intelligent men speak and am pleased when I can follow them."* To them, such passive acceptance might even seem like intellectual engagement.

However, true equality will only be measurable after women have enjoyed full intellectual and social parity for centuries. As long as they live under the oppressive weight of intellectual devaluation, only the strongest natures will break through. Conversely, women suffering from self-aggrandizement often produce subpar work, which reinforces prejudices about women's creative inferiority—prejudices that many are all too eager to uphold.

The strong development of imagination, a trait often inherent to women, coupled with their enthusiasm for beauty—expressed even in domesticity—suggests that proper education could unleash their creative potential in all artistic fields. Creativity requires inner freedom, and once the obstacles and societal suggestions of intellectual inferiority are removed, women's potential for innovation can truly flourish.

The greatest accomplishments come from passionate engagement with a field that deeply resonates with the soul—not from activities undertaken for pragmatic reasons. Dr. Mathilde Ludendorff notes that the areas of interest for men and women differ fundamentally, a divergence observable even in childhood. For instance, a little girl on a train is more likely to observe the faces and expressions of the passengers, while a boy is intrigued by the construction of the locomotive. Girls are more drawn to people than to things. This difference also explains why women, when consumed by love, often deprioritize previously important endeavors.

This focus on people rather than objects represents the most fundamental difference between the sexes. Ludendorff provides a real-world example: a female telegraph operator may use a device for years without ever pondering how it works. A man, however, feels uneasy using a tool whose mechanics are unknown to him. Yet, while he insists on understanding the device, he might work for years alongside superiors or colleagues without any interest in their inner lives or personalities. His focus is purely on their professional output, and he often knows as little about their character as the female operator knows about her machine. In contrast, a woman feels uncomfortable working with someone whose inner nature is unclear to her. Through observation of expressions and behavior, she seeks to discern whether they are genuine or disingenuous. She is often quick to arrive at accurate conclusions, unless strong emotions for the individual cloud her judgment.

This psychological sensitivity makes women particularly suited to fields requiring empathy and insight—psychology itself being one such field. As psychology has historically been dominated by men, it has suffered from significant gaps and limitations compared to sciences that require no psychological insight, such as physics, chemistry, engineering, mathematics, and surgery. These latter disciplines remain the natural and most fruitful domains for men.

By recognizing these innate tendencies and strengths, both men and women can flourish in roles that align with their natural inclinations, contributing to a balanced and harmonious society.

Philosophy, as a domain of thought, is equally accessible to both genders, since the realm of the *Überbewusstsein* (higher consciousness) lies beyond the confines of space and time and can be experienced by both men and women in the same manner. However, the intellectual devaluation of women throughout history has suppressed their philosophical contributions and creative potential.

Science, traditionally the exclusive domain of men, has been constructed through the lens of male thought. Women, beginning in school, are compelled to adapt to this framework, which presents an additional challenge. As a result, women's fields of interest may appear more limited than they truly are, as many disciplines—such as history, ethics, literature, and languages—could also be developed from a uniquely female perspective. The current structure of academia often discourages women, as they must rely on foundations built by men. This can diminish their initial enthusiasm for study and research. Instead of imitating male thinking, women should bring forth their distinct perspectives.

For example, in the study of history, women might prioritize understanding the emotional and psychological connections that shape events rather than focusing predominantly on wars and political milestones. The groundbreaking contributions women can offer in this area are exemplified in Dr. Mathilde

Ludendorff's *Philosophy of History*, which demonstrates how a deep, intuitive perspective can yield profound insights.

Women also exhibit notable aptitude in language acquisition. From an early age, girls tend to develop speech more quickly and articulate themselves more effectively than boys of the same age. This linguistic advantage persists in areas such as writing, where girls often excel. Their heightened sense of beauty and form undoubtedly contributes to this strength.

The feminine yearning for beauty, a deeply ingrained characteristic, is frequently mislabeled as vanity or superficiality—a perspective rooted in an Oriental worldview. The desert, barren and devoid of natural beauty, is inherently hostile to the concept of aesthetics and joy. Consequently, material possessions are valued in such cultures more for their monetary worth than for their artistic or aesthetic appeal.

In contrast, the soul of the Nordic individual is imbued with a profound and enduring longing for beauty. This yearning permeates their existence, making them sensitive to environments that fail to align with their aesthetic ideals. When faced with such discord, the Nordic spirit often seeks solace in dreams that transcend space and time. While this appreciation for beauty may be dismissed by outsiders as mere vanity, it is in fact a divine spark—an innate reverence for beauty that elevates the soul above the mundane and often harsh realities of life.

This aspiration for beauty is not limited to humans but is evident throughout the divinely imbued natural world, in plants and animals alike, all striving for as much beauty as the struggle for survival permits. Life would be impoverished without this sacred impulse toward beauty—without flowers, birdsong, and the grace of well-formed beings. Vanity only becomes a vice when it degenerates into arrogance or pretentiousness. Furthermore, this trait is not exclusive to women; men, too, demonstrate vanity, as evidenced by their penchant for titles, medals, and decorations.

The pursuit of beauty, therefore, should be celebrated as a fundamental and divine human instinct, transcending utilitarian concerns and connecting individuals to the sublime.

Undoubtedly, the predominantly external evaluation of women by men has often led many women to vanity and a desire to please. Since women were primarily valued as sexual beings, they came to view it as their task to enhance and develop everything that would make them appealing to men, often leading them astray into artificial embellishments.

This devaluation of women brought with it numerous deviations and excesses. Men, considering themselves the sole agents of cultural achievement, excluded women from participation—denying themselves the complementary partnership that women could provide. Nature has harmonized the souls of the two sexes in such a way that, where men exhibit greater strengths, women have compensatory advantages, and vice versa.

For example, men are generally more self-assured, as they must be to face life's struggles. They are often more susceptible to indulgence in life's pleasures and inclinations. Women, on the other hand, are more resilient when it comes to enduring physical hardships such as hunger, thirst, and pain. Their concern for the well-being of their loved ones often outweighs their care for themselves. Women frequently accept misfortune and suffering upon themselves to shield others from harm.

Of course, exceptions exist—there are pleasure-seeking and selfish women who, lacking self-discipline, express their pain and whims uncontrollably, sometimes spiraling into hysteria. Rigorous discipline instilled in childhood, as Dr. Mathilde Ludendorff advocates in her book *Des Kindes Seele und der Eltern Amt* (The Child's Soul and the Parent's Duty), is the surest safeguard for both sexes against such uncontrolled behaviors. The inherent altruism of an individual is the best defense against hysteria. The reverence for moderation among our ancestors demonstrates that self-control was celebrated as a virtue of Germanic women.

The pronounced selflessness that enables most women to embrace motherhood with all its sacrifices was, during the Christian era, restricted to the immediate family. This narrow limitation often led women to familial selfishness, wherein their thoughts, feelings, and efforts were confined to their small circle. This restriction of scope inevitably narrowed their worldview.

Even today, the majority of girls grow up within such confines, which stifles their potential and renders them superficial and unreflective. As wives, they often settle into the role of mere "housewives," limiting their focus to the trivial concerns of daily life. The meal plan, clothing choices, and perhaps the activities of neighbors encompass their world. Internally unfulfilled and spiritually unsatisfied, many—tolerated by lenient husbands—become habitual gossipers. The innate need for intellectual exchange, a trait of women with stronger emotional capacities, finds no higher aim, leading to envy and resentment that extinguish the divine spark within the soul.

Alternatively, some women may descend into becoming "domestic tyrants," disturbing the peace of the home with petty disputes over trivialities due to the lack of greater purpose in their lives. Such behavior can be even more repellent than that of a domineering man, as it repays the kindness or weakness of the husband with authoritarian control. Conversely, the husband, submissive at home, often compensates by exerting authority outside.

Our ancestors understood the value of women's maternal instincts. Their empathy, willingness to help, and sense of duty were harnessed for the benefit of the community. The Götterlieder (*Songs of the Gods*) in the *Edda* praise these qualities, describing the women of the Heilberg (*Mountain of Healing*) as "Protective, Sheltering, Healing, Kind, Bright, Radiant, Friendly, and Peaceful."

Dr. Mathilde Ludendorff's insights mark the end of the prevailing indifference among women toward their contribution to the community. A girl raised to embody the national spirit, strength of will, and self-reliance will, as a mother, guide her children in the same spirit. There is no need to fear that this will detract from her feminine grace. "Feminine talent complemented by energy leads to the most joyful expression of womanhood," says Mathilde Ludendorff.

The heroic ancestral soul, characterized by foresight, courage, bravery, and self-discipline in the face of danger, most distinctly sets the Nordic people apart from other races and is their most unmistakable trait. This racial heritage should also be nurtured in young girls.

An education grounded in Dr. Mathilde Ludendorff's psychological insights—one that awakens the best qualities of German heritage while making its weaknesses and faults consciously understood and thus overcome—could, within a few decades, give rise to a divinely proud, pure, and strong generation of men and women. This generation would once again resemble the archetype of our national identity, safeguarded against new paths of decline through their understanding.

This is the purpose behind the *Curriculum of Life Studies for German God-Believing Youth*, which Dr. Mathilde Ludendorff, in nurturing maternal care, has gifted to her people.

CHAPTER

7

THE ROLE & POSITION OF WOMEN IN A NATIONAL COMMUNITY

The abilities of women have, until now, not been utilized by the state in any meaningful way, and this oversight has had bitter consequences. How this can be corrected for the benefit of the people is outlined in the work *"The Woman and Her Purpose."*

Undoubtedly, the role of motherhood remains the most sacred duty of women. However, this role provides a sufficient sphere of influence for only about two decades of her life. Before and after this period, especially for women who can employ external help for household tasks or do not work professionally, there is often a lack of meaningful activity. For young girls, the habit of idleness is just as detrimental as it is for sons of the so-called upper classes. Both genders should be encouraged early on to engage in dutiful work, even if initially this involves small contributions within their family unit. Such habits instill a sense of responsibility, not just toward oneself but also toward a broader community—first the family, and later the nation.

A thorough education in the skills required for managing a household and fulfilling the role of motherhood is still lacking today, despite widespread recognition of its importance as the highest responsibility of women. If German women have nonetheless distinguished themselves in their understanding of maternal duties compared to women of many other nations, it is because of their indestructible racial heritage.

A Comprehensive Education for the Young Girl's Role in the National Community

A young girl must undergo at least one year of schooling that comprehensively prepares her for all the responsibilities of a housewife and mother. This training should include the care of infants and the sick, cooking, sewing, maintaining cleanliness and order, as well as gardening and flower care. Physical training through appropriate sports should be paired with psychological and intellectual preparation for her maternal role. Just as boys are instilled with enthusiasm for defending their homeland, girls must be inspired to embrace their sacred calling as mothers. However, under the Christian notion of impurity surrounding creation, such matters are still entirely avoided. Playing with dolls during childhood remains the only form of preparation for the woman's highest and most sacred vocation.

It is curious that, in an age of racial consciousness, dolls representing Africans and teddy bears are placed in the hands of young German girls, displacing the blonde-haired, blue-eyed dolls. Indeed, there is a calculated method behind this. A child who hugs and cares for a doll of a foreign race has their innate sense of German racial awareness eroded early on. For the preservation of race and nation, nothing is more crucial than a thorough education in racial consciousness. The many unhappy marriages we see today stand as a dire indictment of the state, which has so far failed entirely in its responsibilities in this regard.

A national state focused on the health and renewal of its people will bring about the necessary changes to safeguard the well-being of the population. While commendable laws on hereditary health have been passed, they must be accompanied by a rejection of Christian teachings. Christianity advocates for universal mixing, creating a herd without racial distinctions and paving the way for the inferior to triumph over those ennobled by blood and character. Arm in arm with the Church, no racial renewal can be achieved. Pope Pius XI declared in

1927: "Christianity excludes anti-Jewish opposition, for the Jews are the chosen people of God."

A national and racially conscious education will reverse the declining birthrate without the need for legal mandates. A sense of duty toward one's people cannot be commanded; it must spring from the soul and be freely embraced. It is unreasonable to condemn women for their aversion to childbirth when they were excluded from national matters and silenced by decree. How can women develop a sense of responsibility to bear healthy children for their people when they are prohibited from engaging with the nation's affairs?

The longing for children, which often results in misfortune for unmarried mothers and harsh judgment from their peers, is usually satisfied after the first child. Only deeply maternal women will joyfully accept further motherhood, with all its struggles, concerns, and sacrifices. The image of our ancestors, their affirmation of life, and their pure understanding of the sanctity of creation will serve as the ultimate role model, shielding both men and women from degeneration and immorality.

The awareness that women bear responsibility for the vitality of future generations will protect them from moral degeneration and the use of harmful substances such as intoxicants and tobacco, which damage health and destroy life. History provides ample examples of how the actions and omissions of individuals can ripple through time, influencing even the most distant future.

Just as the national community must ensure proper preparation for motherhood, it must also ensure that women are protected from the demands of dual roles during the period of motherhood. A mother must be free to dedicate herself fully to her sacred duty of nurturing her children, without the added burden of a secondary career. Even so, her role as a housewife involves substantial work. Child-rearing, however, should take precedence over household tasks. Advances in technology now ease the burden of housework and should be embraced by housewives to allow more time for their maternal responsibilities. Yet, it is neither necessary nor beneficial, for mother or child, for a mother to constantly dote on her children. The Germanic tribes knew no indulgent spoiling or constant play with children. Tacitus wrote, *"In every household, children are raised without much fuss."*

Humans value most what they do not possess continuously, and thus mothers should make their time with their children special, allowing it to become a cherished occasion. From an early age, children should be taught independence, enabling them to develop autonomy and self-reliance. Children thrive best in the company of peers, as an adult cannot fully understand the child's perspective. A child's best playmate remains one of the same age group.

When children grow older and seek their own paths, mothers should grant them the freedom to develop and should learn from nature. A mother animal devotes herself to her offspring only until they are fledged and capable of self-reliance. However, some women persist in "mothering" their adult children rather than seeking new tasks or channeling their energies into contributing to the welfare of the community. Forces opposed to the well-being of the people have effectively hindered mature women's participation in societal endeavors, often by ridiculing them as "old maids" or "meddling mothers-in-law." In some cases, this criticism was warranted, as their desire for activity found no outlet other than interfering in the young households of their children. This is the result of a flawed, narrow education that fails to extend beyond the four walls of the home. Proper intellectual development in youth will enable mature women with time and energy to take on higher responsibilities that serve the nation. They will reject the notion of mere "endurance and silence" as unworthy. In nature, only mature fruit is truly valued, and nature should always remain our teacher, for its laws represent the divine order.

Through the joys and sorrows of motherhood, women grow and mature spiritually, making them particularly well-suited to contribute to the state. Many gaps created by the one-sided activities of men could be filled by women's cultural contributions.

Mathilde Ludendorff notes that it is a disadvantage that mothers are often excluded from the teaching profession. A mother could more easily forge the emotional connections with children that are so critical for effective education. Moreover, she would better understand how to present teaching materials in a refreshing and engaging manner. For this reason, women should be involved in the creation of textbooks. It is only recently that efforts have been made to present educational content in ways that elicit interest and understanding in children.

For adolescent boys, the maternal and feminine influence—even in schools—is just as important as the masculine education that complements it for girls.

The contribution of women would also be invaluable in fields such as medicine, particularly in women's and children's healthcare, and in the area of mental and neurological health. Dr. Mathilde Ludendorff, who practiced as a neurologist for many years, pointed out the incomprehensible fact that mentally ill patients were still restrained in "straitjackets" to render them harmless, even at a time when medicine was capable of performing the most complex surgeries. She also criticized the practice of generalizing experiences from individual cases to others without delving into the patient's psyche.

This same error has been made in the field of jurisprudence. Psychological motives are not taken into account. Instead, fixed punishments are assigned for specific offenses, creating a rigid schema or norm. Women, however, tend to approach matters by considering each case individually, assessing its internal connections and motivations. Such an approach would reduce the number of instances where "justice" effectively becomes injustice. It would also be a woman's task to examine the credibility of witnesses. Currently, German courts lack the intuitive safeguarding that women could provide. This is likely because they still practice "Roman law," not Germanic law.

The participation of women would also enrich and deepen historical research, art history, and literature, as well as social welfare and politics. Mathilde Ludendorff advocates for "no more and no less than that women create for themselves a politics that complements male politics, gains significance for the state, and morally permeates the entire political sphere." Thanks to their selfless orientation, women could ensure that the rights of all are considered and that the power ambitions of individuals are limited for the sake of the common good.

To realize these goals, women must first and foremost help themselves. More than male ambition, it is female indifference that acts as a barrier. Women's purely gender-based valuation by men has, over the centuries, caused them to become alarmingly externalized. Women must come to recognize their value to the nation and their shared responsibility in national affairs.

Above all, women need a legal status that corresponds to the dignity of German womanhood. Both genders must rise against a legal system that infantilizes mothers within society as severely as current laws do. The Christian principle that "the man rules because he is a man" underpins all marital provisions in the Civil Code. "The man has the decision-making authority in all matters concerning the shared marital life" (Section 1354, Paragraph 1).

Most women live in complete ignorance of the law. They typically only experience its severity and injustice when they themselves seek justice. How else could a woman endure being rendered legally incapacitated when she dedicates herself to her most sacred task—motherhood? Both women and men must oppose the fact that a woman's signature is not fully recognized because she is deemed "legally incapacitated," equating her status with that of a drunkard or a mentally ill person.

As a result, in many marriages, she assumes the role of the eldest, legally incapacitated child who receives pocket money for her contributions. Under current law, everything earned jointly within the marriage legally belongs to the husband alone. A wife is not allowed to manage her own assets, although a working daughter is. Thus, she is legally subordinate to her own child. In all matters concerning the children, the husband makes the decisions. Even if a woman dutifully fulfills her responsibilities at home, she cannot secure true freedom for outside activities against her husband's will—except to contribute financially, but not for idealistic reasons.

As long as German women endure such a Jewish legal status with indifference, and men feel no shame in accepting it—indeed, even take pride in being "the lord over their wives"—there can be no progress. Progress can only come from a German valuation of women. When individual families return to German values, the elevated status of women, through their morally purifying influence, will extend to society as a whole and demand new jurisprudence. A German judge, Karl Bulling, based on extensive experience in marital cases, concluded that "any form of legal authority granted to the husband presents a serious moral danger for him and is incompatible with the woman's right to freedom in fulfilling her duties."

The freedom of self-development, which even animal mothers enjoy, should certainly also be granted to human mothers. In reality, however, it is often only the man in most marriages who benefits from such freedom. He is regarded as superior due to his supposed experience and self-control, though he is by no means always so. Girls are often raised with this notion as a given. An upbringing that fosters critical thinking and judgment will protect them from unquestioningly accepting everything in marriage from their husbands. Men, too, must be made aware of their faults. Only then can both spouses grow together in marriage, developing and enriching one another. Without stifling each other, they will freely and robustly unfold their personalities, channeling them into positive influence on the family and the community.

The patriarchal marriage, as enshrined in law, has created in Germany a type of woman still praised by even nationalist circles today: the enduring "Gretchen" celebrated by Goethe and sung of in Lamartine's women's songs—the Christian ideal. A meek, obedient, childishly submissive woman who, as a "lowly servant," looks up in reverence and humility to the "lofty star of glory." This is the "Käthchen von Heilbronn" that inspired Kleist. Yet, in him, as in other German poets, there always struggled the ideal of the heroic Germanic woman against the oriental-slavish ideal, allowing a Penthesilea to rise alongside a Käthchen.

The woman who, often still emotionally immature, enters marriage without opinions or judgments of her own and faces a husband who was raised to be independent, may initially not perceive this subordination as degrading, swept up as she is in romantic enthusiasm. Eventually, however, her innate Germanic yearning for freedom will push her toward the development of her own personality. She will form her own opinions and judgments. If these no longer align with her husband's worldview, and if the husband is intolerant and authoritarian, the relationship may break. Having previously encountered no independent thoughts from his wife, he now interprets her emerging individuality as defiance and hostility. He may believe their happiness has been destroyed through her fault, failing to recognize that the assertion of personal uniqueness is part of divine creative intent.

Only the emotionally great and free man will find joy in a wife who is equally free and great in thought. Most men today, however, shaped by their upbringing and environment, are not yet capable of this. A model for them can be found in the great commander who chose for his life partner a great philosopher.

The conflict between the desire for freedom and the preservation of a wrongly founded marriage drives many women to emotional ruin. Some avoid separation or resolution by outwardly appearing to follow their husband's will while secretly circumventing it. Such false morality is even praised as special wisdom, a sad indicator of societal decay.

A German newspaper once published under the headline *"How Do I Deceive My Husband"* the following moral teaching: *"A woman must be an actress to keep her husband's love. She must flatter him, even if it means pretending. She will then achieve everything with him."* The Rebekah of the lentil stew has been achieved. The sacred bond of marriage and the trust it demands have been desecrated. A German woman would rather face the difficulties of separation, even if it presents her with the toughest decisions, than remain the wife of a man who denies her the freedom of intellectual development and activity that he claims for himself without asking her permission.

The healing of love will progress in tandem with the recognition of German womanhood. Mutual respect between the sexes will naturally follow. It will shape German marriage into the ideal as exemplified by General Ludendorff and his wife:

"The wish of every healthy, mature German individual must be to complement and elevate their own nature through a lifelong bond with a healthy, noble, and like-minded individual of the opposite sex. This alone constitutes a true marriage of German kind.

In this marriage, man and woman stand side by side as equals, though differing in essence, as comrades."

"*Love can either awaken or destroy the soul,*" says Mathilde Ludendorff. Just as it is every person's free choice how they develop their soul—whether they choose to soar to great heights or descend into the depths, whether they rise from a misstep in clear recognition to ascend or sink even deeper, shaping themselves as either divine or devilish, thereby creating heaven or hell for themselves and others—so it is also their free will whether they seek fulfillment in love in the lower realms, in fleeting, intellectually shallow connections that lead to physical and emotional ruin, or whether they strive for a soul union that inspires them to the highest heights and a connection to the divine.

Love has the power to awaken the best and strongest qualities in a person, driven by the desire to be worthy of the beloved. But it can also lead to the deepest depravity.

Mathilde Ludendorff also shows the path to healing in matters of love. In her work "*The Healing of Love*" (*Der Minne Genesung*), she writes:

"*Both sexes must learn in their youth that it represents an act of utmost self-disrespect and self-degradation when a person chooses, for the most intimate physical connection, someone who would not even be considered suitable for friendship. A sense of reverence for their highest capacity for happiness must be instilled in people from a young age.*"

The double standard of morality has led men, through early practiced polygamy, to become incapable of sustained passion and deep love, while women—dishonest with themselves—deny awakened love because they no longer possess the consciousness of purity in their desires that our ancestors once held.

Especially among Nordic women, feelings of love and friendship for a man are often entirely free from sexual thoughts. Yet, German men are rarely able to value such favor from women as purely and nobly as it is intended.

Mathilde Ludendorff states:

"*Since the spiritualization of love is much more frequent in women, it is their duty to help men rise above their baser instincts.*"

"*Young women must understand that they can only expect respect from the opposite sex if they serve as role models of moral purity.*"

The mere presence of a woman can elevate the tone of a man's conversation.

However, the noble goal of spiritualized love can only be achieved if women no longer live in intellectual subordination and if marriage is based on racial and thereby spiritual affinity. How can a marriage ever flourish when it unites racially opposed individuals? Their souls respond so differently to the same experiences that harmony becomes impossible.

Most marriages are formed only through superficial attraction or romantic infatuation—not to mention the contractual arrangements of Jewish economics. The essential question—whether the soul of a partner resonates and harmonizes—goes unanswered. These unions often endure later only through inertia or economic necessity, presenting a pitiful picture of bourgeois stagnation.

Physical beauty fades, but the beauty of the soul is untouched by aging. It can grow ever more magnificent until the day it ceases with death, fulfilling its divine purpose: to achieve godly perfection.

The creative purpose of the universe, which the philosopher of the soul, Mathilde Ludendorff, offered humanity through her works on the philosophy of religion, assigns women their highest and holiest role. This role, which women also fulfilled among our ancestors, is the reason why nature endowed them with such a rich and profound soul: to proclaim, nurture, and strengthen the divine in the world and protect it from destruction by enmity toward the divine! This is their highest and holiest destiny.

To fulfill this role, there is no need for priestly garb or ordination, even though some professors are now offering it. Suddenly, people recall that the Germanic woman held the office of divine proclaimer within her people. She is no longer considered inherently sinful or inferior. There is talk of returning this office to her, of making her a "priestess," and it is suggested that she would not even need to don a priest's robe as men do.

However, this gesture betrays fear—fear of the awakening of the German woman. Those who hold onto the priesthood and their spiritual domination over nations are willing to sacrifice male power and superiority to preserve their control.

But the German woman will no longer be deceived. She rejects the rabbinic garb and willingly leaves it to men. If the man possesses a healthy German soul, he will also awaken and cast it off, as the courageous former Catholic priest Franz Griese has done. "Away from Rome and Christ," he calls to the Germans, for whom their Germanness is still their most sacred and highest value.

It is no coincidence that a woman has taken up the fight for the freedom of the German soul. This fight could only begin with a woman because no one has been as maligned by Christian doctrine as women. Therefore, it is their task to carry the banner of freedom in this battle. Only liberation from the spirit of the Orient will restore women to their rightful place in family and society—a place that once ennobled and strengthened the Germanic people.

The robed clergy and their followers may continue to regard women as impure, inferior, and inherently sinful. But the German people will free themselves from all Orientalism. The German woman will not need priestly robes, incense, or other rituals to inspire her family and people with reverence for greatness, nobility, and beauty. She will draw from the deep, pure, and sacred well of her soul, from her experience of divine aspirations toward freedom, truth, beauty, kindness, and love. Then the Germans will learn once again to reject ungodly actions and to love what is divine.

The suffering path of our people will make them aware of the flaws and dangers in our blood and strengthen them in their understanding and resistance to the enemies of the people.

Where the German marriage is realized, the man will no longer need secret male societies to ennoble or elevate himself. The woman will no longer require a confessor who promises her heavenly rewards for humble obedience to her husband's will.

Once our women recognize that their continuous personal subordination is not divinely ordained but rather an Oriental principle of servitude designed to separate them from their people, they will view the role of servant, maid, or plaything as unworthy and immoral. They will become proud and heroic once again.

They will see that their sphere of influence does not end at the doorstep of their home, even though the home remains their sanctuary—a sanctuary that once existed when our ancestors knew no churches or prisons for the soul, a sanctuary whose peace they regarded as sacred.

With higher and broader goals, German women, in partnership with men, will fight for the healing and preservation of their people. They see around them the deep spiritual and economic distress of their nation—how secret international powers are depriving their families of the means to live, how young Germans can no longer build marriages, how the sound of children's laughter has vanished, how the youth, hopeless and burdened with worries, withers away—without work, or in work, without wages. The current hardship sweeping across the earth is certainly not "divinely willed" but deliberately engineered.

It depends on you, German woman, today. They knew well why they humiliated you for centuries and why they continue to seek to keep you in servitude, dependency, and intellectual immaturity. They do not want you to understand the interconnections of global events.

The thread of eternity spun by the Norns has been severed. Uprooted from the past, you no longer understand the present. They know the immense strength for fighting and enduring that your soul holds.

In your pure hands rests the fate of your children, of your people. Will it, through your help, rise again to its highest and purest blossoming, becoming a source of renewal for the world through its moral and cultural heights, as it once was—before foreign influence crossed the Alps—or will Germany, and with it the world, descend into chaos?

In the proximity of the death of divine world order, it was a German woman who solved the riddle that had been encircled and questioned for millennia, providing answers to the questions of the meaning of existence, becoming, and death. Fierce hatred flares against her from all those who see their thrones toppled and their oppressive strongholds, which for centuries have tormented and enslaved the human spirit, collapse. Death is not an enemy but a co-creator of the human soul, which owes its divine awareness to it—the triumph of the will to immortality. The intellectual work of Mathilde Ludendorff will endure long after all the slanderous and deceitful voices have been silenced, forgotten, and self-destructed.

A fearful premonition of what the awakening of German women could mean trembles through the conspirators of the world. The field marshal of the World War has taken up the fight against them. He drives them out of their strongest positions. His goal: the unity of blood, faith, law, culture, and economy, which means the salvation of all peoples and the free development of their divinely willed national identities. You, German woman, are called upon to help lead your people to freedom and prosperity, to guide its soul back to itself and to the German view of God. Rise to your task!

The field marshal and the philosopher provide you with the tools for the sacred struggle of your people. Use them. Then you will not raise your children to be slaves and sacrifices for Rome and Judah. Instead, you will give your people the heroic lineage that—honorable and defensive—fully realizes the German essence, ensuring the preservation of the people and the divine.

Thus, a free and pure people will live on free soil!

www.ingramcontent.com/pod-product-compliance
Lightning Source LLC
Chambersburg PA
CBHW041934260326
41914CB00010B/1286